Instructional Decision-Making
A Guide to Responsive Instruction

INSTRUCTIONAL DECISION-MAKING
a guide to responsive instruction

Thomas M. Sherman

Virginia Polytechnic Institute
and State University
Blacksburg, Virginia

EDUCATIONAL TECHNOLOGY PUBLICATIONS
ENGLEWOOD CLIFFS, NEW JERSEY 07632

Library of Congress Cataloging in Publication Data

Sherman, Thomas M
    Instructional decision-making.

    Bibliography: p.
    Includes index.
    1. Teaching--Decision making. 2. Individualized
instruction. I. Title.
LB1027.S4665   371.39'4   79-23611
ISBN 0-87778-140-0

Printed in the United States of America.

Library of Congress Catalog Card Number:
79-23611.

International Standard Book Number:
0-87778-140-0.

First Printing: March, 1980.

3 11 (Se Barberd tabr 20.85

Preface

Classroom teachers, instructional developers, and school administrators all face the problem of determining what opportunities and experiences will best help students to learn. These decisions are complex, because they involve so many variables and require so much information. In addition, these decisions must be accurate, since the students' success as learners may depend on the quality of the decisions.

Obviously, everyone involved in education makes a large number of decisions every day. Some of these are very pervasive and touch all students, such as decisions about classroom atmosphere or philosophy of instruction. Other decisions may affect only one or perhaps two students. In any event, all of these decisions should be made to facilitate learning and be informed, conscious, and purposeful.

Being a good decision-maker is not easy for most teachers or instructional developers, due to the volume of data which must be analyzed. For example, it is necessary to know the aptitudes and interests of students, the content to be taught, and the parameters of the instructional environment in order to arrange instruction to meet the learning needs of students. In addition, teachers must be aware of the options available to them from which alternatives may be chosen. Teachers must also be familiar with recent data from empirical research and from developments in learning theory which may facilitate decisions. All of these areas of information must be synthesized into each instructional decision. This is certainly a very demanding responsibility, which requires a good deal of sophistication to be done effectively.

The purpose of this book is to provide guidance in the process of organizing and managing information into effective instructional decisions. Since the decisions required are so complex, one requirement for effective decision-making is that the complexity be reduced to a manageable level. In responsive instruction, this is accomplished through the use of *systems thinking* and the systematic construction of instructional decisions. Responsive instruction also includes specifically identified decision-points; each of these is examined in terms of alternatives available. Finally, responsive instruction is based on a belief that if students are given the necessary conditions, then they will learn. In other words, the instruction must be responsive to student learning needs. Instruction is made responsive by teacher decisions to manipulate instruction in a manner consistent with these needs.

The major goals of this book, then, are to describe the basic elements of a responsive approach to instruction; to identify a structure or framework for making instructional decisions; to identify the instructional decisions which must be made; and to review the information available on these decisions.

This work is the product of the ideas and efforts of many people. Jane L. Ellison provided major assistance in formulating and developing the basic ideas which serve as the foundation for this approach to instructional design. William H. Cormier provided not only a strong beginning for the development of the ideas but also much needed moral support for articulating them. Terry M. Wildman helped to flesh out several areas where I was unsatisfied with my own ideas. Bea Martin provided much help in typing and clarifying my thoughts. Janice and Bill Sherman, more than anyone else, gave me the time and encouragement to write and think. I am grateful to each of these friends.

T.M.S.

Table of Contents

Instructional Decision-Making
A Guide to Responsive Instruction

Part I: Introduction

1

Responsive Instruction

Introduction

It is possible to develop a lengthy list of important functions teachers perform in facilitating classroom learning. There is, however, one theme or consistent responsibility running through all tasks teachers perform which really makes the teacher essential. Regardless of the task involved, the teacher must make *decisions* about the task; this includes decisions about what materials should be used, the methods by which a lesson will be presented, how feedback should be given, the best method for encouraging students, and so on, for every classroom activity. The central and unique contribution that a teacher makes to successful classroom learning is to insure that the best instructional decisions are made to facilitate that learning.

All teachers must make a large number of these decisions. Even before entering a classroom, the teacher must decide what content will be taught, what resources will be needed, and how students will be grouped, among other decisions. Once in the classroom, the teacher must make decisions relative to such events as the best procedure for answering questions, how much time to spend on a particular example, and whether to respond to a question or continue a lesson. And, once the lesson is completed, it is necessary for the teacher to decide which students have learned and how well they have learned. In fact, teachers are responsible for making so many decisions that it does not seem unreasonable to think of a teacher as a decision-maker whose major task is to make decisions which result in students learning effectively.

Responsive instruction is an approach to developing, delivering, and evaluating instruction in which these teacher decisions are considered *systematically*. Basically, the logic of this approach is that if a teacher is aware of the possibilities available to him or her, the probability of selecting an appropriate alternative is much higher than if he or she is unaware of them. To establish this range of alternatives, it is necessary to examine the instructional milieu in order to identify the features which the teacher may control. Once these features are identified, it is then necessary to examine a process for determining how to choose the best alternative. This is essentially a decision-making process which emphasizes the role of teacher action as it relates to student learning.

In this chapter, we will look at responsive instruction from several vantage points in order to provide some background and basic information. We will begin by briefly tracing some of the research and thinking on instruction to see where responsive instruction fits within these general trends. We will also examine a definition of responsive instruction in order to gain a full understanding of what it is and how it can be helpful to teachers. Finally, we will spend some time discussing decision-making as it relates to responsive instruction. When you have completed this chapter, you should have a good idea of what responsive instruction is and be able to identify salient reasons for using this approach.

Developmental Background and Rationale

There are three major influences on education which have contributed to the development of responsive instruction. In order to help you understand the reasons for and utility of responsive instruction, we will review these three ideas or influences. They are: individualized instruction, aptitude-treatment interaction research, and the development of systematic approaches to decision-making.

Individualized Instruction. Individualized instruction has the longest history of the three influences mentioned. There is probably not a teacher, student, administrator, parent, or person involved in education in the United States today who has not heard of individualized instruction in one of its many forms. Practically every teacher has wished to have more time or fewer students in order to attend more carefully to individuals. This is clearly a very popular idea and has been so for centuries. As evidence of current interest, one need only scan a title index of professional journals in education and psychology. Literally hundreds of articles on individualized instruction appear every year in such journals.

Why is this an appealing idea? It appears that the basic reason is that almost every educator recognizes that people are different. In recent years, more and more emphasis has been placed on the different ways in which people learn. As a result, many educators have been looking with serious reservations at the traditional instructional practice of teaching a group of students in a single way. After all, if students do learn differently, just as their physical appearances are different, then we cannot expect every student to profit equally from a single instructional strategy, such as a lecture. Another way of looking at this issue is in terms of the distinction between adaptive and selective instruction. For centuries, formal education was an expensive commodity with a luxury orientation. For the most part, only the very rich or extremely adept students were "educated"; others were expected to take jobs at an early age. As a result, it was quite important to carefully select those students who were to occupy the scarce positions available for students in educational institutions. Education became selective; that is, ways of separating or selecting good students from poor students were developed and utilized. This was ordinarily done by giving tests to see who had already learned the most; those who had learned a great deal were retained, the others released.

There are several implications that this selective orientation toward instruction has for education. First, it implies that some students cannot learn well. Those who cannot are "selected out" of the educational system. This may be done by failing these students or by simply allowing them to drop out. Second, it places the major responsibility for learning on the student. Whenever one instructional method is considered "the best" method to teach a lesson, the students are implicitly given the responsibility to respond to this "best" method and to learn the lesson taught. Obviously, there is no accommodation of individual differences in how students might learn best.

Adaptive instruction, on the other hand, postulates that because students learn differently, all students will not learn to their maximum potential from a single instructional method. That is, different people may learn the same things differently. For example, a mathematics class which involves the use of abstract symbols in concept development may be most effectively taught to two different students using different instructional approaches. One student, who can handle abstract concepts well, may learn a formula or concept through a verbal explanation. However, another student, who is unable to deal with abstractions adroitly, may find a verbal explanation confusing and frustrating. This student, however, may be able to learn the same concept if it is presented through the use of concrete objects. Thus, instruction is adapted to the learning needs of the student by adjusting instructional methods to fit the student's learning style.

It is also frequently the case that the same person will learn differently depending upon what he or she is asked to learn. For example, a person who is adept at verbal learning may handle oral or written explanations of ideas quite well. However, if the person were required to learn a manual skill, a written explanation might be inadequate. To successfully master a motor skill may require a demonstration or model which could be imitated.

Aptitude-Treatment Interaction Research. The second influence is the growing body of research most frequently referred to as aptitude-treatment interaction (ATI) research. This research seeks to identify the differential responses of learners to various instructional strategies. In other words, because one student possesses a certain characteristic or aptitude, he or she may learn more effectively from one instructional strategy or treatment than another student who does not possess that characteristic. In one study, for example, Dowaliby (1971) concluded that students who were highly anxious (trait) performed worse when they were presented unstructured or student-centered instruction (treatment). On the other hand, these anxious students did much better when presented more structured instruction. Based on this study, we might conclude that student anxiety appears to interact with the degree to which instruction is structured. At present, there are relatively few generalizations that can be made reliably concerning the interactive effects of different instructional programs on different people. However, there is sufficient evidence to support the idea that such interactions *do* take place and that these interactions can be important determinants of what an individual learns.

ATI research has emphasized the need to carefully consider the instructional actions engaged in by a teacher. That is, since the instructional activities employed by the teacher constitute the treatment given to students, these strategies must be carefully selected in order to maximize the probability of successful learning by individual students. It is clear, then, that any particular teacher action may bear a direct causal relationship to what is learned by the student. As a result, it is possible for teachers to accept greater responsibility for what students learn and do not learn.

Systematic Decision-Making. The previous discussion leads to a need for coordinating these developments and ideas into a useful and practical frame of reference for teachers. With recognition of the existence of individual differences, as well as the differential effects of teacher action on student learning, the question raised is, "How does a teacher know what to do to provide the best possible learning experience for each of his or her students?" Unfortunately, there is no magic answer here, because the teacher must examine the instructional situation and students involved in order to make such a decision. It is clear, though, that the decisions the teacher makes can be critically important for student learning. What we can do is examine the process that is used to arrive at these decisions in order to identify the best process for making instructional decisions. The development of effective decision-making processes is the third major influence on the development of responsive instruction.

Actually, there is relatively wide agreement on what constitutes an optimal process for decision-making. Let us begin this review of the decision-making process by discussing a key question associated with making decisions. The question is, "How is a good decision distinguished from a poor decision?" Many times the response to this question is, "By the outcome." That is, if the outcome was what was desired, the decision was a good one; if the desired outcome was not achieved, the decision was not good. There is no doubt that the outcome is an important factor in evaluating a decision. However, in an enterprise as complex as instruction, where judgments must be based on tentative and sometimes sparse data, we need to look at more than just the outcome. We also need to look at the *process* the decision-maker uses to arrive at the chosen course of action.

To illustrate this point, consider the following. One teacher uses a film to make his students aware of the complex issues associated with the beginning of the Civil War. He decides to use a certain film because he remembers that the film was helpful to him in identifying relevant issues when he studied the Civil War. Another teacher also uses a film for the same purpose, after considering a lecture and a class discussion. However, this teacher selects the film because she has data on her students indicating that many of them require some visual information to reinforce verbal information. In addition, this teacher is aware of research conducted with the film indicating that the manner in which the issues are presented in the film facilitates student understanding. Here we have two teachers making essentially the same decision. However, the process each used was quite different. The former used only his own recollection, while the latter considered several alternatives and employed information on her students and some empirically gathered data to make her decision. Regardless of the outcome achieved, the decision by the second teacher appears to be more informed and carefully considered. It is the use and consideration of information and data which differentiate the quality of the second teacher's decision. In other words, the second teacher employed a more reasonable decision-making process; the use of such a carefully selected process is extremely important for consistently making good decisions when complex issues are involved.

The process most widely recommended by researchers and writers on decision-making contains five components (see D'Zurilla and Goldfried, 1971). These are (1) general orientation, (2) identifying intended outcomes, (3) generation of alternatives, (4) decision-making, and (5) verification. These components are presented in a logical sequence in that activities in the preceding component naturally lead to the activities in the following component. While this is a logical sequence, it is not invariant, and shifts forward and backward are to be expected when demands for additional information arise or it is discovered that important activities have been overlooked. In this sense, the decision-making process is meant to be a general guide for systematically making decisions rather than a formula to be rigidly followed.

Let's take a brief look at each of the components in the decision-making process described, emphasizing how each relates to making instructional decisions. The first component, general orientation, concerns the manner in which the decision-maker approaches the decision situation. Essentially, this means that the teacher must recognize that teaching regularly requires a multitude of decisions and that these decision situations can be effectively mastered. It also means that teachers must be able to recognize when decisions are necessary and that they resist the temptation to act impulsively or by habit. Thus, teachers must be aware of when it is possible for them to make decisions, must have carefully considered these decision-points, and must be prepared to implement a decision-making process.

The second component of the decision-making process is identifying intended outcomes. The major tasks of the teacher here are to specify clearly the intended outcomes of the decision in concrete terms. That is, the teacher must carefully consider what outcomes are desired and analyze and structure these outcomes into a useful framework. This component also includes the acquisition of whatever additional information will aid in making the decision. Assessment data on students, empirical evidence, logic, and anecdotal data are useful as aids in making instructional decisions. In other words, this component represents the development of a firm analytic statement of what the teacher

wishes to accomplish and the accumulation of sufficient supportive information.

The generation of alternatives component can be engaged in by
several teachers or just one. The intent is to sufficiently explore
alternative routes to the desired outcomes so that a good choice is
likely. In general, the more alternatives that are available to the
teacher, the higher the probability for an optimal match of an
alternative with an instructional situation. Creativity and utilization of existing resources are goals during this component of
decision-making. This may involve discussing the situation with
other teachers, uninhibited day dreaming, and/or extensive reading
of professional literature.

Decision-making is the component of the process in which the
various alternatives are considered and the most probable for
success selected for implementation. All data generated earlier
must be relied on in order to select the best alternative.
Essentially, this is done by analyzing student assessment data,
empirical evidence, personal information, etc., and selecting the
alternative which appears to be the best. Obviously, this is a
judgmental decision, because teachers have no foreknowledge of
outcomes. However, careful consideration of all information and
important situation factors should lead to more frequently
successful decisions.

The final component is verification. A characteristic frequently
noted in effective decision-makers is a concern for knowing the
results of the decision made. Thus, an attempt is usually made to
follow up each decision to determine if the decision made was the
best or, if not, how it could have been improved. Teachers also
need to review and evaluate the effects of their decisions. This
may be accomplished by examining student learning and by
reviewing other alternatives.

The important feature of utilizing a systematic decision-making
process for teachers is that this process may increase the
probability of making consistently good decisions. Attention to
this decision-making process allows for careful study and analysis
of decisions, which has two advantages. First, it is possible to
study and improve upon the way individual instructional decisions

are made. As a result, a teacher can continually improve the manner in which he or she makes decisions. Second, each decision can be examined as a learning opportunity for the teacher. Whether the outcome is positive or less than what was expected, a teacher operating from a systematic framework can isolate problems and avoid making the same error again.

Each of these three areas—individualized instruction, aptitude-treatment interaction research, and decision-making—has implications for instructional design and delivery. Clearly, if students have different learning styles which affect their ability to learn, these student differences should be considered by teachers. Similarly, if we can expect instructional activities to differentially affect students, we must be able to match students and instruction in order to achieve the maximum probability for learning. And, to identify and coordinate the interactions between unique student abilities and instructional activities require a multitude of conscious, carefully considered decisions by teachers. It is clearly a large task to organize and coordinate all these factors. In fact, it appears to be next to impossible without a well-organized framework to guide the planning and delivery of instruction.

Responsive instruction is a framework which provides the necessary organization to include all these factors. Responsive instruction is basically a decision-making model which focuses on the instructional actions engaged in by a teacher. That is, instruction is conceived of as an active intervention by a teacher into student learning. This intervention may take many forms. The only limitation is that the teacher must possess some control over the instructional milieu in order to actively provide instructional assistance to a learner. This control must be exerted over environmental factors in the instructional milieu.

Let's examine this point in further detail. It appears that we must accept that learners are different and that instructional events will affect learners to a greater or lesser extent, depending upon the different characteristics of the learner. We can't *change* a student who learns best via a demonstration into a student who learns well from a verbal presentation. However, we *can* change the instructional procedures, so that whatever is to be learned is presented through a demonstration. In other words, the instruction can be designed to be *responsive* to the way students learn, rather than selecting students out because they do not learn.

In order to be responsive to student learning styles, the teacher must take some action to adapt instructional procedures to the student. This kind of adaptation involves manipulation of features in the instructional environment to make that environment responsive to identified student needs. That is, since the student cannot be modified, the only avenue open to a teacher is to arrange everything around the learner to help him or her learn. As teachers, it is necessary that we manipulate or arrange the instructional environment to promote learning or make learning easier for students. We cannot force students to learn, nor can we inject "learning"; we facilitate learning by making what we want students to learn more attractive to them. (As an alternative, some teachers will promote learning by making "not learning" very unattractive; that is, by failing students, ridicule, or threats of other dire circumstances. However, this approach is not helpful to students who experience problems mastering what is to be learned.) In practice, learning is positively facilitated by the teacher taking some action to change the classroom. That is, the learning environment is altered in some way by adding, eliminating, or rearranging classroom variables to aid learners to acquire the skills, values, or knowledge desired. Teachers can employ a wide range of activities to manipulate the classroom to facilitate learning.

When considering the range of possible alternative actions that teachers might take to promote learning, it is necessary to examine the learning environment to determine what actions are *possible* for a teacher. It is possible for a teacher to act to facilitate learning only to the extent that the teacher has control over the learning environment. For example, many teachers feel that the student's "home life" has a strong influence on what and how much a student learns. In fact, there are some data which indicate a relationship between socioeconomic status, parental attitudes toward school, and the student academic achievement. However, the teacher has little or no control over these "home-life" variables. That is, the teacher cannot modify socioeconomic status and rarely can change parental attitudes toward school. Thus, while this is an important issue in whether a student learns, the teacher lacks sufficient control to act upon the factor.

There are a number of important factors upon which the teacher *can* act to facilitate learning. That is, in any learning environment, there are variables which the teacher can control and manipulate to improve the possibility of students learning. *Teacher control, then, refers to the ability of the teacher to act upon features in the learning environment for the specific purpose of fostering student learning.* These factors represent the specific decision-points which a teacher must address. By examining the learning environment, we can identify those variables and, as a result, define the range of alternative actions available to a teacher to help students learn.

In responsive instruction, 14 of these decision-points or instructional variables which are possible for a teacher to act upon or manipulate have been identified. These 14 variables appear to apply to all learning environments and include all possible teacher alternatives. In essence, then, what we are doing is identifying the total range of instructional alternatives available to teachers in terms of the actions that may be taken to promote learning. We have also concurrently identified major decision-points for instructional development.

To illustrate this concept, let's take a look at one of these variables and how a teacher could manipulate it to promote learning. The variable of time to learn or "rate" of learning is a dimension which prominent educators (e.g., Bloom, 1974; Carroll, 1963) have pointed to as crucial. Time to learn refers to the amount of time which is made available to a student to master the skills, values, or concepts being taught. This variable can be manipulated by teachers in several ways. For example, all students may be given the same amount of time to learn, either in terms of how much instruction is available or in terms of how much time they have to produce evidence that they have learned. Bloom (1974) reported that he frequently found that the difference between students mastering content and failing was the amount of time they were given to learn. Here is an instructional variable over which the teacher can exercise control and manipulate to be responsive to student needs in order to facilitate learning. The need for a teacher decision is obvious here; the teacher must provide either more or less time, according to the learning needs of each student.

Responsive Instruction

Responsive instruction is a systematic approach to making instructional decisions about the optimal arrangement of instructional variables to promote learning. The focus of this approach is on the systematic and purposeful arrangement of the instructional setting in order to be responsive to individual student learning needs. To facilitate understanding of the concept of responsive instruction, we will examine the above definition and identify the 14 instructional variables which comprise teacher options and decision-points in developing an instructional program.

Let's begin by dissecting the definition by important phrases and concepts. The first key phrase is *systematic approach.* This implies that instruction is conceived of as an integrated and orderly activity with each component of the instructional process drawing upon previous components and having implications for all other components of the process. As a result, instruction must be considered first as a total entity with all components interacting with each other. This is in contrast to a series of isolated and independent steps. In practice, this means that instructional activities range backward and forward within the framework rather than proceeding in a step-wise fashion, particularly during instructional development. The developer of instruction must maintain a flexible and open attitude characterized by constant reexamination of previous activities and ramifications of subsequent activities for prior decisions. In effect, each component of the development process is a specific decision-point at which a variety of instructional alternatives must be examined and evaluated. Whatever alternative is decided upon must be selected in the context of the total instructional program. In addition, the use of the term "process" in association with "systematic approach" implies that instruction consists of a series of identifiable components. This has the benefit of providing specific instructional activities to which instructional decisions can be directly tied. This means that the teacher can focus instructional development activities on these decision-points to gather and utilize necessary decision-making data.

The next important phrase is *making instructional decisions.* The teacher is considered to be a decision-maker. Casting this decision-making responsibility in the framework of the responsive instruction model provides two benefits. First, the teacher can identify the specific points in the development process where major decisions must be made. As a result, the teacher can be alert to and aware of when decisions are necessary. The teacher develops a general orientation or readiness to make these decisions. Second, the teacher can become aware of the nature and implications of specific decisions. All necessary data can be gathered to support the needed decision because of the specificity provided by the model. This allows for more systematic acquisition of assessment data on students, of empirical data, and utilization of logic in making these decisions. The teacher, as a result, becomes a more informed decision-maker, who is able to bring a wealth of information to each decision-point.

The next phrase in the definition is *optimal arrangement of instructional variables.* Two important implications need consideration here. First, the use of the term "optimal arrangement" implies that it is possible to identify some instructional procedures that will work better than others. However, it is recognized that perfection is not possible. In addition, since most teachers must work with groups of students, it is incumbent upon them to decide on instructional procedures which will be best for the group as a whole. This is not to say that each student should not be treated as an individual. However, within the limitations of time and space, each teacher must decide which instructional actions on his or her part will be of greatest benefit to most students. In this sense, the teacher must consider the individuals who are members of the group as well as the group as a whole. As an example, a teacher may decide to concentrate on individualizing evaluative feedback rather than instructional procedures. Such a decision would necessarily limit time devoted to content delivery in favor of maximizing the amount and quality of feedback to students.

The second implication has been alluded to several times. It concerns "instructional variables." The focus of responsive instruction is on identifying ways that teachers can act on the instructional environment to make the environment responsive to learner needs.

Finally, the phrase *to promote learning* implies the goal orientation or purposefulness of responsive instruction. The goal is to promote learning, and all decisions regarding arrangement of instructional variables are oriented to promote student learning. Clearly, the teacher must be aware of when learning occurs and when failure to learn occurs. When failure is the outcome, teacher decisions must be reexamined in order to search for a better arrangement of the instructional variables. Even when an acceptable level of learning is the result, the teacher needs to review instructional decisions to identify the most salient decisions and those which could be improved upon even further. As a result, the teacher is constantly aware and informed of the outcomes of his or her decisions and is able to replicate success and avoid repeated failures as a "promoter" of learning.

A good bit of the discussion to this point has centered around the responsive instruction model and the 14 instructional variables or components of the model. It is now time to unveil this model and provide some explanation. Table 1.1 is a list of components of the model.

There are two major features of this model which you should note. First, the instructional process is broken into five major developmental components indicated by bold face type. These five components are: Planning Instruction, Structuring Learning, Delivering Learning, Evaluation, and Remediation. The second feature is that within most major components are sub-components. These sub-components represent the various specific components or instructional variables which require

Table 1.1

Components of the Responsive Instruction Model

Planning Instruction

1. *Intentions*

2. *Assessment*

Structuring Learning

3. *Goals*

4. *Content of learning*

5. *Learning processes*

6. *Objectives*

Delivering Learning

7. *Time to complete objectives*

8. *Time to deliver objectives*

9. *Message channel*

10. *Instructional strategies*

11. *Space*

12. *Grouping*

13. **Evaluation**

14. **Remediation**

---

teacher decisions in instructional development. It is here that teacher decisions in selecting the best alternative from identified possible alternatives are made to optimize student learning. Put another way, by selecting an appropriate course of action at each of these decision-points, a teacher can make instruction responsive to student learning needs. In the following discussion, we will address each of these components in terms of the major developmental categories.

The development of instruction necessarily begins with planning. This category includes teacher activities which directly relate to beginning the process of instructional development. The first sub-component in this category is labeled intentions. Teacher action in this component consists of the determination of what is to be taught, resulting in general statements of instructional intent. For example, in a curriculum planning session, a single teacher or group of teachers may decide that every student needs to acquire certain general abilities. These may be statements such as, "Every student should develop the ability to think critically" or, "Students should appreciate art." Such decisions as these provide a baseline of general intent which serves as a foundation for future developmental activities.

The next sub-component, assessment, is where current student achievement is compared with these stated intentions. In effect, assessment is the process of measuring the gap between where students are and where they should be relative to the learning intentions. Teacher activities in this component involve gathering data about students which will guide present and future decisions. This can include student data on dimensions, such as previous experience, achievement, learning style, background, interests, etc.; in other words, any data which describe student characteristics important for instructional decisions should be gathered. In addition to these student data, available research should be reviewed to identify possible alternatives as well as opinions from other members of the educational community regarding methods, practices, goals, etc. Following completion of these activities, the teacher should ask if all relevant data have been gathered. If not, additional searching and data-gathering would be indicated. If the answer is yes, then proceed to the next developmental category. This is a major decision-point in the instructional development process. Representative questions or issues for this and subsequent major decision-points are given in Table 1.2.

The next major category is structuring learning. Once a general idea of what is to be taught/learned is established and the necessary decision data are gathered, what is to be learned must be organized in a meaningful way. It must be specific enough to guide both learning and instruction. Whether one argues in favor of a discovery learning approach (Bruner, 1966), an expository approach (Ausubel and Robinson, 1969), or some other form of organizing learning, there appears to be sufficient evidence to indicate that learning is facilitated by instruction which is developed in some organized fashion rather than randomly presented. This category includes the specific teacher activities which result in structuring or organizing what is to be learned.

The first sub-component is goals; this component follows as a logical sequel to previous decision activities. Goals are a relatively specific network of statements which define the gap between what is intended and where students are. In most cases, goals will grow directly out of intention statements but will be more specific and suggestive of what students are to learn. In addition, all goals should be considered and integrated into a logical and related sequence. This often requires refining broad goal statements into subgoals resulting in an outline of what students are expected to learn. These goal statements provide the necessary specificity the teacher needs to identify intended outcomes.

Content of learning refers to the analysis of goals into specific types of learning by classifying the content that students are to learn. It is essentially the process of further analyzing goals into more manageable instructional statements. Learning processes, the third sub-component, involves decisions about what students must learn to meet the goals and what kind of conditions must be present to facilitate their learning.

Once these structuring decisions have been made, a final decision-point remains in this major component—objectives. It is here that the learning outcomes are specified in detail to describe

Table 1.2

*A List of Suggested Questions for Major
Decision-Points Identified in the
Responsive Instruction Model*

---

1. Have all relevant data been gathered which are needed to plan instruction?
   Are sufficient data available to make decisions relative to the expressed intentions?

2. Is the learning properly structured to facilitate student learning?
   Are the goals and objectives consistent with the planning component?
   Do additional goals need to be added?
   Are objectives clear?

3. Does the planned delivery correspond with stated intentions and student learning needs?
   Does the planned delivery utilize available resources to maximum advantage?

4. Is the evaluation selected consistent with student learning styles and the learning program?
   Does the evaluation allow for identification of learning problems?
   Did students learn as expected?

5. Was the learning program satisfactory for student learning needs?
   Did the student have sufficient time?
   Was the proper message channel available?
   Was the best strategy available?
   Did the grouping patterns suit the student's learning style?
   Were sufficient and proper resources available and utilized?

6. Was the learning structured appropriately for the student?
   Were the proper goals stated?
   Was the content appropriate?
   Were the correct mental processes chosen?
   Was the level of abstractness correct for the student?
   Were the objectives appropriate?

7. Was the learning properly planned for the student?
   Were the intentions appropriate for the student?
   Was the proper and necessary data gathered and utilized correctly?

---

what students should be able to do as a result of their learning. The decision about how to specify objectives frequently determines how well students understand what is expected of them, and, obviously, for this reason, it is quite important. When each of the sub-components in this category have been addressed, a general categorical review should be conducted centering around a question, such as, "Are the objectives consistent with student needs, goal statements, logic, assessment data, empirical evidence, etc?" If the goals appear to be sufficient to meet the instructional needs, the development process should proceed to the next category.

Delivering learning includes all the teacher actions which result in direct teacher-student interaction. Time to complete objectives involves teacher decisions about how much time students should be given to learn or to meet learning requirements. Time to deliver objectives, on the other hand, requires a decision on how long students may or should interact with specific learning activities or materials; learning pace would be an important consideration here. Message channel is the sensory modality selected to convey the learning program. A decision to include one sense—hearing—or several—hearing, sight, touch, etc.—is involved here. The next sub-component is instructional strategies, which are the specific activities a teacher may choose to effect student-learning interaction (e.g., lecture, discussion, programmed materials, role-playing, etc.). Space and grouping follow instructional strategies. Space is the component in which decisions about the physical arrangement of the learning space are made. This includes utilization of space as well as equipment within that space to promote student learning. Grouping refers to the way in which students are assembled for learning; teacher decisions are necessary to determine if students should be alone or in small or large groups during learning experiences.

When the delivering learning category of development activities and decisions has been completed, it is again necessary to review these decisions. At this point, a major review should be conducted around a question, such as, "Does the learning program correspond to the planned intentions, the structure of learning desired, and students' needs?" If the planned learning program appears to be satisfactory, then the next major category, evaluation, can be initiated.

Evaluation includes all the activities in which a teacher engages to determine the effects of the learning program. Teacher decisions are needed to determine such issues as how to evaluate (e.g., immediately or delayed), who to evaluate (e.g., all students or individually), and what to evaluate (e.g., concept formation, knowledge, or skill development). These are critical decisions, which are reflected in the accuracy with which the teacher is able to measure student learning. One purpose of evaluation is to be able to identify those students who have learned successfully. A second purpose is to be able to identify students who have not mastered the learning in order to provide remedial learning experiences. A review should be conducted as with other categories to insure that the evaluation procedures are appropriate for the learning program and the students.

Remedial experiences make up the last major developmental category, remediation. Remediation is a relatively complex set of teacher activities requiring a good deal of teacher analysis and decision-making. The purposes of remediation are to identify the reasons for insufficient student learning and to formulate alternatives to previous decisions. Instructional problems indicated by insufficient student learning may be the result of a single or a combination of incorrect teacher decisions. The identification of where decisions need to be altered involves a complete review of the development process with a specific reference to procedures within each major category. Because remediation is a complex process, instructional planning must include remediation as a regular developmental function. When the problem-point is identified, the student is recycled in light of the newly acquired information. Obviously, a new set of decisions would need to be generated to remediate the learning problems.

This model provides some specific and useful benefits to the teacher/decision-maker. First, the points in the development process where decisions must be made are identified. As a result, the teacher is able to pursue both practical and empirical information as well as to apply logic and reason in generating an informed decision. Second, the development process is presented in an orderly fashion, which facilitates systematic consideration of instructional alternatives and the implications of these alternatives. Third, because major decision-points are identified, the teacher is able to focus data-gathering on specific areas of particular prominence for the students involved.

To take advantage of these benefits and to facilitate instructional decision-making, several kinds of information are required. First, the teacher needs to be informed about the special and unique characteristics of his or her students. It is only with this knowledge about student learning needs that instruction can be tailored to be responsive to these needs. Second, the teacher needs to know what empirical research is available and what this research indicates in terms of particularly successful teaching methods. Third, the teacher needs to know what alternative methods are available in order to choose the instructional method which will best serve the students involved. A teacher with this kind of information should be in a much better position to make an informed, practical decision about the "best" alternatives to match student learning needs with instructional procedures. The remaining chapters are meant to supply a large portion of this information. Each chapter covers one or more components of the responsive instruction model and includes a review of empirical data where available, an identification of needed decisions, some possible alternatives, and decision-making procedures.

The major purpose of this book is to help teachers become better instructional decision-makers. To do this, the components of the instructional process where decisions are required will be identified. This should help to develop a general orientation toward the need for decisions and facilitate identifying additional areas where decisions may be required. Procedures are also suggested for gathering data on students and how these data may be used to choose specific instructional methods is described. Along with this, there will be additional information on the identification of intended instructional outcomes based on logic and empirical research. This should also facilitate the generation of alternative instructional procedures. In other words, it is intended that the reader will become informed about instructional decision-making in order to make instruction responsive to student needs.

The actual decisions, however, must be made by a teacher for his or her students in a specific educational situation. No one can prescribe such decisions in advance or present a "sure-fire," "all-purpose" method for success. The information and evidence must be weighed and analyzed by the teacher involved. In effect, there is no "best" method; to the contrary, there are many methods, any one of which may be the "best" for the teacher and students in a particular situation. The selection of this "best" method for a particular situation will be facilitated by utilizing the information contained in the following chapters within the organizational framework of responsive instruction.

References and Suggested Readings

Ausubel, D.P., and Robinson, F.G. *School Learning.* New York: Holt, Rinehart, and Winston, Inc., 1969.

Berliner, D.C., and Cohen, L.S. Trait-Treatment Interaction and Learning. In F.N. Kerlinger (Ed.), *Review of Research in Education.* Volume 1. Itasca, Ill.: F.E. Peacock, 1973.

Bloom, B.S. Time and Learning. *American Psychologist,* 1974, *29,* 682-688.

Bruner, J.S. *Toward a Theory of Instruction.* Cambridge, Mass.: Harvard University Press, 1966.

Carroll, J.B. A Model of School Learning. *Teachers College Record,* 1963, *64,* 723-733.

Cronbach, L.J., and Snow, R.E. Individual Differences in Learning Ability as a Function of Instructional Variables. Final Report. Office of Education, OEC 4-6-061269-1217, 1969.

Dowaliby, F.J. Teacher-Centered vs. Student-Centered Mode of College Classroom Instruction as Related to Individual Differences. Unpublished Master's thesis, University of Massachusetts, 1971.

D'Zurilla, T.J., and Goldfried, M.R. Problem-Solving and Behavior

Modification. *Journal of Abnormal Psychology*, 1971, *78*, 107-126.

2

Foundations of Responsive Instruction

Instructional decisions are based on a number of factors. These include basic beliefs about how learning occurs, general notions about the purpose of education, previous experiences which have led to success or failure, and the possibilities which the instructional situation provides. At present, numerous sources are available which describe a variety of basic and applied considerations or theories about learners and education. These various positions often present conflicting ideas of what happens when someone learns. Regardless of what one believes relative to how learning occurs, the teacher faces the problem of how to implement or put these beliefs into practice. As a result, while teachers may have a theory of learning to guide them, they may not have a good framework for putting these beliefs into practice in a systematic manner. In effect, a practical plan is needed to organize and analyze the instructional situation so that instructional decisions are consistent with basic beliefs about learning and education.

The ordinary starting point for any theoretical approach to promoting learning is with basic assumptions about either learning or education. Responsive instruction is neither a theory of learning nor a philosophy of education. Responsive instruction is a move away from theorizing about learning, memory, and education to an analysis of instruction and the possibilities for instructional actions which exist in any instructional setting. These possibilities exist regardless of the theoretical position held. Thus, it should be possible to utilize the basic tenets of any learning theory or educational philosophy within the framework of responsive instruction.

Responsive instruction provides a systematic decision-making framework which includes opportunities for accommodating a variety of different notions of how learning occurs and philosophies of what education should be. This is possible because all teaching occurs within the context of an instructional situation. Whether one believes learning results from high or low structure, is intrinsically or extrinsically motivated, is guided, or directed, or whatever, the instructional situation must be arranged to conform to these beliefs. Responsive instruction provides the framework for making instructional decisions which conform to any theoretical position.

A teacher who believes that students learn best by discovery approaches will take actions to organize an instructional situation to facilitate discovery of subject matter. Another teacher, who believes in a more tightly structured or deductive approach, will attempt to arrange the instructional situation to promote such learning; however, these actions would be quite different from those of the first teacher. What each teacher has in common is that both need to be able to analyze and organize the instructional situation in order to, first, identify what alternative actions are available to them and, second, determine which of these actions are consistent with the theory and philosophy they hold. It is only after one recognizes what actions are possible that it is feasible to systematically choose the specific course of teacher action most consistent with a theory and philosophy.

This is not to imply that responsive instruction is not predicated upon several basic premises. It is obvious from the discussion in the first chapter that there are several factors which have contributed to the formulation of responsive instruction. Similarly, there are several influences which have affected the design and structure of the responsive instruction model for instructional decision-making. These influences fall into two general categories: influences from learning theories and influences from instructional design.

Learning Theory Influences

While responsive instruction is a framework for making decisions about instructional action and not a learning theory, clearly it would be foolish to ignore the great advances made in understanding the learning process made by learning theorists and researchers. The learning theory influences most directly affecting responsive instruction tend to be associated with all theories rather than specific to any one position. Of course, different theories suggest different methods or procedures for instruction. However, the responsive instruction framework is designed to emphasize the decision-making function for implementing these various methods, rather than specifying exact procedures. The first influence from learning theory, which appears to be widely held, is the uniqueness of learners. That is, because the experience or perception of experience is unique for each individual, they will differentially react to any additional experience. Every human being sees new experiences in the context of his or her previous experience, thus no one reacts exactly the same to any single event as any other person. These reactions may be very similar or widely disparate, but they will never be precisely the same. Second, there is wide agreement that feedback is closely associated with learning. Perhaps this is most clear in the theories of cognitive theorists, particularly information processing theorists, such as Miller, Galanter, and Pribram (1960) and cyberneticists, such as Landa (1977). However, behaviorists and developmentalists also highlight the role of feedback in learning.

These influences serve as basic assumptions for responsive instruction. The assumption that learners are unique implies that one must be aware of the characteristics of each learner. A teacher cannot be responsive to student needs if he or she is unaware of these needs. It also implies that the teacher must have the capability to routinely and systematically follow reactions by learners as these occur. The teacher must be able to tell where learners are throughout the learning process. This places heavy demands on the teacher.

The assumption regarding the necessity of feedback also places demands on an instructional design. Important considerations center around the type of feedback to be given, the quantity of feedback, and the timing of feedback. Again, different theories prescribe different approaches to guide teacher action. The fact that the role of feedback is widely recognized, though, indicates the importance it holds for learning. Feedback serves a controlling function in the sense that information about any action will allow for the individual to adjust or modify behavior in future action. The more systematically or regularly such feedback is included in the instructional design, the more effective the instruction is likely to be. The theoretical assumptions held about how learning occurs will guide teacher decisions on the nature and form of feedback which should be provided to students.

The sum of these influences leads to the conclusion that effective instruction results from carefully considering the student as a complex and changing entity. The instruction must be able to accommodate not only the complexity of learners, but also the continuous change which occurs as humans learn. Students must be considered not only in terms of entry behaviors or initial competencies but also in terms of their reactions to the instructional program.

Instructional Design Influences

In the past ten to 15 years, there has been a great deal of interest and research in the general area of instructional design. This is reflected not only in the research literature, but also in the volume of books and articles published which include the terms instructional design, systematic instruction, management of learning, and so forth. Three major influences from this area have direct bearing on the design of responsive instruction. The first of these is the frequent utilization of systems ideas in the design of instruction. This includes not only the idea of systematically designing instructional experiences, but also the concept of a holistic approach to conceptualizing and implementing instructional programs. The second consistently discussed influence is the need for planning and organization in the development of instruction. The third major influence is the impact of the increasing availability and utilization of instructional technology.

This includes machine technology, such as the use of audio and visual techniques, as well as the use of human performance technologies, such as behavior modification.

The utilization of systems ideas is the first influence. Flow-charts and systems diagrams often are employed to describe both the sequence of instructional planning activities and the flow of action during instruction. This type of presentation has several benefits in that a complex process (instruction) can be represented in a concise and descriptive manner. All major components of the process can be identified in such a way that the role of each component is clear. When human behavior—in this case, teacher action—is conceptualized in this manner, it is possible to place all behaviors in a relatively exact temporal and spatial sequence. There are, as a result, both theoretical and practical advantages. In addition, the nomenclature is widely recognized and accepted, which is an aid to understanding. The system is considered as a single entity designed to result in a desired outcome. Churchman (1968) refers to this as a "mode of thinking" which constitutes the substance of the systems approach. It requires a careful and wide-ranging analysis of goals and the impact of every action both individually and as a contributor to the system. The system is a whole entity, the outcomes of which may not be totally in line with expectations without a holistic consideration of the system and all its ramifications. One reason postulated for the failure of many so-called systems is that they have been developed utilizing only the systems nomenclature without the *substance* of the systems approach, the holistic approach to problem-solving (see Sherman, 1978).

The second major influence coming from the general area of instructional design is the emphasis on planning and organization. In the past, teaching was often prepared and delivered in an *ad hoc* or proverbial manner. Methods and content were selected on the basis of general acceptance or tradition. Frequently, teachers were prepared to teach by being given a series of prescriptions for action when specific situations arose. As a result, teachers were generally not equipped to visualize the scope and sequence of learning as a continual process. Perhaps the ultimate articulation of the pitfalls of this approach is Landa's (1977) notion of "He couldn't figure it out because he couldn't figure it out." To the contrary, instructional designers recommend that instruction be planned to take into account as many contingencies as can be expected. Planning, then, involves consideration of students, resources, outcomes, and the context of instruction. Instruction must be organized into a logical sequence of activities which will lead to student learning with a reasonable probability of success.

Planning and organization are obviously closely related activities. Planning usually centers on the allocation and use of resources while organization "increases stability by reducing any uncertainty about what is to be accomplished. It also increases the likelihood of being able to predict the actual outcome" (Davies, 1973, p. 9). Davies (1973) lists three functions of organization: "coordinating resources and effort," "dividing work and function among participants," and "using a hierarchy of authority and responsibility" (p. 9). Effective planning and organization enable the teacher to control and regulate instruction. That is, with good plans and sound organization, the teacher is able to monitor student progress relative to achievement and, based on these data, adjust instructional procedures to meet new instructional demands. The teacher must design a situation in which he or she can establish positive control over what occurs during instruction.

The result of this second influence has been to place a great deal more attention on outcomes (student learning) than on teaching as the benchmark for effective instruction. Instruction has been more widely recognized as a complex process with definite goals. Rather than teaching being considered as "presenting the material," instruction is viewed as a series of activities engaged in by the teacher to achieve the purposes stated for the instructional program. These activities include planning instruction, structuring instruction, delivering instruction, and evaluating instruction. The overall impact is to place the major burden for facilitating learning on the instruction rather than expecting students to learn because content material is available.

The third area of influence is instructional technology. Instructional technology is not an easy concept to pin down. There appear to be two general classifications, however, which fall into the category of instructional technology. The first includes the whole range of utilization of machinery—mechanical and electronic—in instruction. The explosion of developments in recent years, particularly in electronics, has provided educators with an almost undreamed of capability for presenting content to students. A generation ago, only two methods were widely used: print and verbal presentations. Today, however, most teachers have a wide selection of methods available to present content, including film, videotape, computers, slides, television, and so forth. The availability of these technological modes of content presentation has generated interest and research in utilization. For most of the new technologies, we have no definitive answers as to which to use, to the best advantage, with what students, in what way, and when. This is not surprising considering the short time most have been available. However, the very availability of this new equipment has opened many options which were heretofore unthinkable. For example, it is now possible for teachers to redefine their roles in instruction in order to maximize their particular talents. Teachers need not feel bound to the role of information or content presenter. They may define their role as learning facilitators, or as evaluators, or as problem-solvers, or in a number of other ways because the burden of content presentation may be discharged through the use of the new media technologies. Thus, these new technologies have opened up many new possibilities for teachers to select from in designing instruction.

The other general classification of instructional technology includes those techniques for influencing human behavior which have such a solid and extensive research base as to be classified as part of a technology of human behavior. In general, "the defining characteristic of a technology is that it provides a methodology for application of scientifically derived principles" (Sherman and Smith, 1976). In general, for a technology of human behavior, this refers to the application of learning research to deliberately shape the learning of students. There are a number of contributors from different theoretical and philosophical perspectives which have made contributions to this technology. These include behavioral scientists, structuralists, and others. However, the clear implication of these technologies is that it is possible for teachers to positively affect student learning in a regular and reliable manner. Thus, teachers have powerful tools at their disposal to promote learning, which should obviously be incorporated into an instructional design.

A framework for instructional decision-making must allow for the incorporation of all of these influences. More precisely, what is needed is an organizational framework for systematically considering the implications of these influences within an instructional design. In addition, while these described influences are far-reaching, we have not reached the point where we completely understand the nature of learning. We know learning is a complex process and that influencing learning (teaching) must be considered a complex task. However, since we fall short of being able to predict the exact impact of any action or series of actions on student learning, we also must be able to involve the "art" of teaching in instruction. That is, many instructional decisions must be based on intuition, experience, and the "feel" of the situation, as well as on scientific findings. When possible, science should be employed to increase the probabilities of success; when science fails us in making decisions, whatever means available must be employed in deciding upon a course of teacher action.

In both cases, science and art, the probability of success is greatly enhanced if decision alternatives are systematically considered. Decision considerations are more fruitful when grounded in the reality of what is possible than if based on "what would be nice if only . . ." Thus, responsive instruction is essentially a systematic approach to the consideration of the finite range of actions possible to teachers. These possible categories of actions are included in responsive instruction as components in a systems approach to instructional decision-making. This provides the decision-maker with an opportunity to consider not only each category of action, but also the relationship of that action to all other possible actions. Thus, instruction can be considered from a holistic perspective. It is also possible for each individual to utilize his or her unique philosophy and theory of learning as a basis for determining what course of instructional action will be most productive in a given situation. In no case is it possible to specify an absolutely correct course of action; this is the major reason teaching is such a challenge. It is also the reason humans are necessary for the instructional process to be effective. It is only through careful analysis and evaluation that good decisions can be made. What is clearly possible is for a teacher to analyze an instructional situation and to make a decision regarding the best course of action relative to the given resources, students involved, and possible alternatives. Responsive instruction provides the framework for making this type of decision.

The Instructional Exchange

One final concept needs to be articulated before examining the specific components of the responsive instruction framework for instructional decision-making. This is the concept of the instructional exchange. An instructional exchange is composed of three elements: the student, the content, and the teacher. Instruction is essentially bringing these three elements into interaction. This interaction is important because the success of instruction is dependent upon the manner in which student, content, and teacher are brought together. Thus, the purpose of instruction is to plan, initiate, facilitate, and evaluate the interaction of these elements.

The first element is the student or learner. As previously discussed, the student comes essentially as a "given" with relatively permanent characteristics. We also know that the learner is a complex human being who is the product of a multitude of unique, interactive experiences. It may appear contradictory, but an instructional design must take advantage of the learner's stable characteristics in order to promote change. That is, the learner comes to instruction with a background of knowledge and experience as well as habits and learning style preferences which must be used by the instructor to make decisions about future learning needs and the best means to satisfy these needs. The learner, then, must be understood in order for appropriate decisions to be made relative to content and teaching. It is the learner who is the major source of decision-making data for all instructional decisions, since these decisions must be responsive to learner needs.

The second element, content, refers to "what is to be learned." As noted earlier, instruction is a purposeful activity; the content, in effect, defines the purpose in terms of what students are to learn. Many times, content is considered a given in that it is thought to be a relatively set body of knowledge or subject-matter designation. However, it must be recognized that what a student needs to learn relative to any body of knowledge will vary in relation to what the student already knows and how fast he or she learns. There is, as a result, the good possibility that content will have to be adjusted to student characteristics. In order to be responsive to student needs, content decisions must be based upon student background, readiness, interests, abilities, etc. In addition, it may be necessary to arrange the sequence and structure of content as students learn, since the requirements of a novice learner are likely to be different from one who is experienced. Content must be considered a complex component of the instructional exchange.

The third element is the "teacher." "Teacher" is used in a generic sense rather than strictly referring to specific actions occurring between a student and teacher. That is, "teacher" refers to any planned activity that will result in the learner coming into contact with the content. This may include actions, such as a lecture or discussion, as well as reading assignments, use of programmed texts, independent study activities, etc. To make teaching responsive to student needs, it is necessary to consider student characteristics and content so that the means selected are appropriate for both. The goal is to select teaching strategies which optimize the probability that students will learn the chosen content. Such decisions, to be responsive to students' needs, must be based on student characteristics, content distinctions, and resources available.

What appeared as a simple notion of an instructional exchange may now appear to be a complex concept. We have the interaction of three elements, each of which is complex, coming together in such a way that the complexity of the interaction is greatly increased. The point, here, as has been previously stressed, is that instruction is a very complex enterprise. Decision-making in the face of such complexity is challenging, since not only the complexity of each element must be considered, but also the interaction possibilities must be carefully thought out and planned. A traditional way to deal with this complexity is to ignore it; that is, to treat all students as if they were the same, or to treat content as if it were immutable, or to consider the job of teaching as a given (i.e., always use a lecture), or all three. The result, however, will not be responsive to student needs. In effect, no decisions are made, because no alternatives are considered.

To be responsive to students in the context of an instructional exchange requires recognition of the complexity of students as well as the large number of alternative courses of action available to teachers relative to content and instructional methods. Decisions about the arrangement of content and teaching must be made on the basis of educational philosophy, theory, and a knowledge of what is possible. As with any complex enterprise, such decisions are more likely to produce favorable results when all the factors involved are considered systematically. The responsive instruction decision-making framework provides for this kind of systematic consideration of instructional variables.

References

Churchman, C.W. *The Systems Approach.* New York: Dell Publishing Co., Inc., 1968.

Davies, I.K. *Competency-Based Learning.* New York: McGraw-Hill Book Company, 1973.

Landa, L.N. *Instructional Regulation and Control.* Englewood Cliffs, N.J.: Educational Technology Publications, 1977.

Miller, G.A., Galanter, E., and Pribram, K.H. *Plans and the Structure of Behavior.* New York: Holt, Rinehart, and Winston, Inc., 1960.

Sherman, T.M. Teaching Educators to Use the Systems Approach:

An Instructional Analysis. *Educational Technology,* 1978, *18,* 40-47.

Sherman, T.M., and Smith, B.V. Application of Behavioral Technology to Small-Group Discussion with University Students. *Instructional Science,* 1976, *5,* 93-105.

Part II: Planning Instruction

3

Intentions

The first step in instructional decision-making is to decide what is to be taught and learned. This may sound obvious and elementary, but, in fact, it turns out to be a crucial and somewhat complex component in designing instruction. The decision relative to what will be taught and learned must be carefully considered in order to insure that what is intended becomes a reality. This decision rests on several important factors. First, the content must be appropriate for the students; it is impractical to teach something that is irrelevant or that students are not motivated to learn. Second, the content must be "learnable." That is, the students must have the necessary aptitudes, foundation knowledge, and other preparation necessary to master the intended content. The major decision-making problem is where to begin the process.

To begin with a specified body of content may result in the selection of content not appropriate for students. One cannot determine the suitability of content for students without a data base for making decisions. On the other hand, it is necessary to have some content goals in mind in order to determine if students are ready to learn. That is, student abilities must be assessed in the context of what they are to be taught.

The logical beginning point is a general statement of what is intended in terms of what is to be taught and learned. This general statement provides a rough basis for gathering data about students. After these student data have been acquired, the original intentions statements can be refined into more specific goal statements, which are directly responsive to student needs.

The first component in the responsive instruction model is planning instruction. This planning is initiated in the sub-component, intentions. *Intentions are broadly framed purpose statements which define the limits of instructional activity.* This definition has two important implications. First, the idea of *broadly framed* implies that the intentions are general and non-specific. At this stage of development, it is important to establish only general purposes for instruction. The second important notion is that these intentions *define the limits of instructional activity.* In other words, intentions statements identify what will be excluded from consideration from the instructional program. For example, if the intentions are to teach American History, a relatively well-defined body of content is defined. This intention excludes European History, Ancient History, and so forth, except to the degree that each contributes to American History. Similarly, an intention to teach arithmetic focuses development activities within a relatively defined domain, excluding content such as geometry, trigonometry, etc. The intent here is to begin to limit the focus of attention to a recognizable entity which can be carefully scrutinized later in terms of the learning included.

Procedures

How does a teacher or instructional designer begin to establish intentions? The first step is to identify a need. This knowledge or ability deficit is frequently noted by school systems in the results of standardized tests. It may be, for example, that students in the school system read with a significantly lower level of comprehension than should be expected. Essentially, a need is present when there is a difference between the way things are and the way they should be.

During this phase of instructional planning, the concept of need is relatively vague and general. At a later point in the planning process, needs will have to be formalized and specified. The intentions sub-component includes decisions which set the parameters for future planning.

The establishment of intentions is often overlooked by instructional designers as an integral part of the decision-making process. As the initial step in instructional planning, intentions, in many ways, set the stage for all future decisions. Thus, it is important that this phase of the process be consciously implemented in order to start the decision-making process in the right direction. Let's review the functions of the intentions sub-component.

First, intentions define the parameters of the instructional content. This has been mentioned previously, but some additional explanation may help to clarify this function. One of the first steps is to determine a general organization of what is desired for students to learn. This may include content areas, such as history, math, etc., as well as processes, such as problem-solving or the scientific method. Establishing boundaries of this sort allows for further thinking and discussion to focus on the issues of interest. A second function of the intentions sub-component is to establish a philosophy which will guide the instruction. This is particularly critical when several teachers or programs are involved. It is not necessary that everyone agree on a single philosophy. However, it is important to recognize the philosophy which is influencing instructional decisions. Thus, it is important for all to be aware and conscious of the beliefs upon which decisions are based. This, of course, is equally important whether a single teacher or many are involved.

A third function of this sub-component is to establish some agreement on the need for an instructional program. This will be particularly important when new or unusual instructional programs are being proposed. In situations where existing courses are being redesigned or extended, need is not such an important issue.

A fourth function of this sub-component is to establish a conceptual framework for the instruction to be planned. This is a relatively important notion which, if carried out effectively, can ease future development. The idea is to construct a holistic concept of the instructional program. This may be done in several ways, but it involves a visualization or imagining of what the instructional program will look like when it is completed. Obviously, this cannot be a fixed product. Rather, it should be a general conceptualization of how the major pieces of the instructional program will fit together. These "mental pictures" can guide productive thinking and decision-making by focusing on these initial developmental steps.

A final function of the intentions sub-component is the opportunity to explore intentions. This may appear redundant, but open discussion of what is intended often brings out many ideas regarding the purposes of instruction. This exploration should include consideration of how the intended instruction fits into the overall educational plan. In addition, customary or routinely expected intentions should be examined. These include intended general outcomes, such as the ability to participate in a democratic society and the development of prevailing social values. The expectations of the school system should also be included in the examination of intentions. The idea is to explore as many areas of intention as possible that are relevant to the planned instruction.

What ingredients are needed to make the establishment of intentions a productive and useful exercise? It appears that several general areas should be represented. Before looking at these, however, we should make clear that this process is one which can be engaged in by a single teacher or instructional developer or by a group of individuals involved in the development of instruction.

What information is needed to establish intentions? The first necessity is content expertise. That is, either the instructional developer or another person must possess familiarity with what is to be taught.

A second necessity in establishing intentions is an awareness of general educational requirements mandated by legal authorities or by custom. Almost all instruction occurs in a larger educational context; that is, a specific instructional experience is a part of a plan to produce "educated" students. Particularly in publicly supported education, state and local school systems require students to have specific experiences which are a part of this larger context. It is important that these requirements be included in establishing instructional intentions, since the instruction must satisfy these requirements. Sources of mandates of this sort come from state and local government laws and regulations. The instructional developer must be aware of these mandates to define what must be included in the planned instruction.

The third source of requirements similar to those which are mandated is custom. Frequently, school systems will have emphases which are accepted by the local community and expected to the same degree as legal requirements. These customary requirements are frequently somewhat difficult to define, since they are traditional rather than explicit. Examples of these expectations are that a high percentage of students will attend college, or that human values will be emphasized, or that all instructional experiences will have a vocational orientation. Clearly, these expectations, even though not legally mandated, will have an impact on the design of instruction.

The fourth factor which should be included in establishing intentions is expertise in related outcomes. Rarely is content competence the only outcome sought from an instructional program. Related outcomes are sometimes articulated and sometimes not. They are almost always present. Teaching students to be good citizens in a democracy is an example of an outcome associated with most public school instruction. This outcome is as important as content related outcomes and deserves equal attention in the instructional planning process. If such an outcome is not identified as an intention, then it is unlikely that it will be systematically planned into the instructional program. It is essential, then, that during the intentions sub-component *all* intended outcomes be identified so that each may be included in the subsequent planning activities.

The fifth ingredient in the process of establishing intentions, which may serve to increase the effectiveness of identifying intentions, is to seek a variety of opinions. This should be done whether a group or a single teacher is involved in the intentions planning. The purpose is to subject the intentions to a brief review by qualified individuals in order to verify the adequacy of the intentions. This is also a good opportunity to receive suggestions from reviewers about beneficial changes in the instructional intentions. Sanders and Cunningham (1973) recommend the involvement of such expert opinion early in the development process in order to insure that the intended outcomes are appropriate. Obviously, experts should realize that intentions represent a very early stage of instructional planning and not a final product. A variety of opinion, however, can serve to test many of the assumptions made by the instructional developer early in the development process and thus avoid problems later. This review by experts should probably be conducted in a relatively informal manner with a straightforward request for an opinion about what is intended in the specific context in which the instruction will be delivered.

Review of Research

A number of sources are available which document the efficacy of conducting activities similar to what have been labeled as establishing intentions. Churchman (1968), in describing the systems approach, discusses the necessity of considering the overall objectives of a system at the outset of the planning process. By such consideration, Churchman indicates that the values associated with an enterprise can be examined along with consideration of purposes and long-range and immediate outcomes. When this kind of thinking is done at the beginning of the planning process, it is possible to make decisions early about whether to go forward with the project, how it may be altered or, perhaps, even if the project should be abandoned. In effect, the planner can begin to develop methods to "optimize" the total effectiveness of the system (Churchman, 1968, p. 23).

The major question in designing an instructional program relates to the need for the program. That is, the instruction must serve some purpose which is unmet. Gagne and Briggs (1974) state that the "perceived need" (relative to instruction) usually falls into one of the following classes: "(1) a need to conduct instruction more effectively and efficiently for some course which is already a part of the curriculum; (2) a need to revitalize both the content and the method for some existing course; or (3) a need to develop a new course" (p. 216). This appears to be a relatively comprehensive statement which defines the beginning point for the process of determining instructional intentions. Such needs usually surface as a result of the perception by someone involved in an educational program that the program is not adequately responsive to the needs of students. Frequently, the initial indicators of such instructional failure are relatively informal misgivings and are anecdotal in nature. As such misgivings increase, it becomes necessary to more formally study the perceived inadequacies and to attempt to define them more clearly.

There is another way, more direct and clear, in which the need for instructional development arises. This is when a new curricular component is mandated by legislative or administrative authority. For example, it may be mandated that every student be involved in a formal program which teaches vocational decision-making. If this type of instruction was previously unavailable, then a complete instructional program must be designed. Even when such a need is mandated, a needs assessment is necessary to further refine the need into realistic intentions.

Formal needs assessment procedures can be quite elaborate and time-consuming. There appears to be a good deal of controversy among practitioners about the efficacy of these needs assessment procedures (e.g., Melton, 1977). The criticism generally centers around the value of spending so much time and effort documenting relatively obvious needs. Regardless of the intensity of the needs assessment procedure employed, there do appear to be some advantages in considering needs when establishing intentions. Burton and Merrill (1977) indicated that the following three benefits accrue from a needs assessment: (1) a focusing on salient problems, (2) a justification for focusing on some needs and not others, and (3) the provision of valuable baseline information against which subsequent changes in student performance can be assessed. The ultimate value, however, may be that consciously attempting to assess needs may so sensitize the instructional planner that more care is taken in establishing intentions for instruction. In other words, there is a greater likelihood of developing an instructional program which is responsive to student needs.

How should the teacher/instructional developer proceed in

conducting a needs assessment? This is not an easy question to answer. Burton and Merrill (1977) indicated that there was no research available which identified a "best" procedure for determining needs. The problem, then, becomes one of choosing a procedure which best suits the specific instructional situation. Let's reformulate this issue in terms of what a needs assessment should accomplish. There appears to be relatively wide agreement that needs assessment should identify the discrepancy between what is and what should be or what is desired. Bradshaw (1972) listed four kinds of needs. These are (1) normative needs, which occur when an individual or group is performing at a lower level than an established standard; (2) felt needs, which occur when something is desired which doesn't exist; (3) expressed needs, which occur when demand is greater than supply; and (4) comparative needs, which occur when one segment of a population receives a service another segment does not. Burton and Merrill (1977) added a fifth need to this list, anticipated or future needs, which occur when a demand is projected into the future.

The teacher/instructional developer should be aware of these different types of needs and assess their relevance to the specific instructional design project under consideration. Some other guidelines or suggestions for needs identification have appeared earlier in this chapter. In summary, these include:

1. Involve as many people as practical in the process of establishing intentions. Of course, these people should be relevant to the process but should probably include teachers, students, experts, etc.
2. Share intentions statements with others who may have information to contribute.
3. Keep in mind that the intentions are tentative and very general. They are always subject to change when new information becomes available.
4. Be open to the full range of possibilities when establishing intentions. Do not eliminate any reasonable or desirable intention because it appears to be impractical or has not been included ordinarily by others.

Keep in mind that the purpose of intentions is to establish a basis for further instructional decision-making. To make decisions at this point in the planning process which will preclude future decisions may short-change the instruction in terms of responsiveness to student needs. With this in mind, however, it must be recognized that no single instructional program can be all things to all students. Thus, it is necessary to limit the range of intentions to a manageable set of expectations. This is often a delicate balance; and it is sometimes a frustrating struggle. In most cases, however, the struggle is worth it if the resulting instruction genuinely is responsive to student learning needs.

Alternatives

The generation of intentions for instruction can be done in so many ways that it is difficult to list and describe alternatives. Decisions on how to proceed with establishing intentions should be made relative to the situation. Using the Gagne and Briggs (1974) classes of perceived needs mentioned earlier, how extensive or elaborate this process should be depends on the class of need involved. For example, if the instructional design is to meet a need to make instruction more effective or efficient for a course which is already part of a curriculum, establishing intentions may be a relatively simple process because the intentions for the course are already fairly well-established. In a case like this, establishing intentions would be mainly validating (and, in some cases, discovering) previously articulated instructional intentions. The process may consist of seeking assurance that the intentions previously established are still current. Another objective would be to determine if any new intentions should be added or existing ones deleted. This can be done by surveying authorities, fellow teachers, students, and others associated with the instruction to be developed. When there is a wide consensus on the intentions, this alone may be enough to establish intentions in order to move to other phases of the design process.

When the second class of perceived need is involved—the need to revitalize both content and method for an existing course—a more formal and extensive process may be necessary. In this case, decisions must be made relative to the best procedures to use to reach consensus and to identify conflicting opinions. The opinion of a broader spectrum of individuals may need to be considered as well as the relation of the instruction to other instructional components of the curriculum. The best beginning point in this process is probably to articulate the current intentions of the instruction to be "revitalized." Following this, the relationship with other curricular components should be examined and specified. At this point, experts can be consulted about the appropriateness of the current intentions. It is necessary that the intentions be examined in the context of other related instructional experiences.

A decision must then be made about how the intentions should be modified. Whatever is determined, these newly derived intentions should then be presented to a larger audience, including those involved in courses which precede and follow the instruction under modification. Frequently, a change in the intent of one course or instructional sequence will precipitate similar revitalizations or create the need for these revitalizations in other courses. The major suggestion here is to involve as many people as practical in order that some consensus is reached on what these intentions should be. This can be done formally and/or informally through the use of questionnaires and interviews. However, the decision on how elaborate this process should or can be again depends on the judgment and decisions of the instructional developer. It is necessary to carefully consider the context in which the new instruction is to be placed in making decisions about this process.

When a new course is to be developed, careful consideration should be given to a number of issues in a relatively systematic way. First, the major impetus for developing a new course should be examined. This involves seeking out the source from which the need for the new course arose. There are a number of possibilities for such sources, such as teacher perception or belief, new legislation, and community pressure. Whatever the source, the rationale for the new course should be understood. Second, the way the new instruction will fit into the existing curriculum should be explored. This will necessitate the involvement of other teachers, school officials, and frequently, school community members.

As with the other classes of need discussed, the level of formality and extensiveness of these efforts depend to a large degree on the context of the instructional situation. Thus, it is the instructional developer who must make decisions about who to involve, how much to involve others, and to what extent the resulting information should be utilized. The purpose of these efforts is to establish intentions for future instructional development which are in line with student needs.

Instructional intentions form the foundation for all subsequent instructional design activities. Thus, it is crucial for the intentions to be established with sufficient clarity so that they reflect the real needs of students. Unfortunately, there are no quantitative methods for determining whether intentions are accurate or not. This depends on the level of awareness the instructional developer gains and his or her willingness to be responsive to student needs. It is a component of the instructional design process which requires carefully considered and thoughtful decisions.

Summary

Intentions are relatively general statements which limit the focus of instructional design activities. Intentions should be developed to set the purpose for the instructional program and provide a framework for all subsequent instructional decisions. Intentions statements should be carefully developed on the basis of a solid review of needs and include all relevant needs. Decisions about intentions must be carefully developed through a process of review and revision of proposed intentions so that a consensus is reached on the general purposes of the instructional program.

References

Bradshaw, J. The Concept of Social Need. *New Society,* March 30, 1972, 640-643.

Burton, J.K., and Merrill, P.F. Needs Assessment: Goals, Needs, and Priorities. In L.J. Briggs (Ed.), *Instructional Design.* Englewood Cliffs, N.J.: Educational Technology Publications, 1977.

Churchman, C.W. *The Systems Approach.* New York: Dell Publishing Co., Inc., 1968.

Gagne, R.M., and Briggs, L.J. *Principles of Instructional Design.* New York: Holt, Rinehart, and Winston, Inc., 1974.

Melton, R.G. Applications of Needs Assessment in the Public Schools: Three Case Studies. *Educational Technology,* 1977, *17,* 36-41.

Sanders, J.R., and Cunningham, D.J. Structure for Formative Evaluation in Product Development. *Review of Educational Research,* 1973, *43,* 217-236.

4

Assessment

Once the intentions for instruction are determined, it is necessary to see how students measure up to those intentions. Assessment is the process of comparing students with instructional intentions. However, assessment involves more than just comparing students to general statements about the purpose of an instructional program. Assessment as the second sub-component of planning instruction includes all activities related to gathering information necessary for making future decisions in designing instruction to be responsive to students.

Assessment is the process of gathering decision-making information about students. This is a general definition which needs further explanation to be meaningful. Remember that the goal of responsive instruction is to make instruction conform to the learning characteristics of students. To do this, we need to have a great deal of information about student characteristics which teachers can utilize to manipulate the instructional environment. That is, we need student information which indicates the optimal arrangement of the instructional environment, given particular students.

Rather than present all assessment techniques at this point, specific assessment procedures will be discussed as each sub-component is presented in succeeding chapters. This will tie assessment procedures directly to the relevant information for each component as it is presented in subsequent chapters.

This chapter will include a general discussion of the importance and utilization of student information. In addition, some guidelines will be given for making decisions about what information to gather.

Assessment and Decision-Making

Making good, conscious decisions in teaching requires information about students. With this information, teachers can arrange instructional features to maximize learning opportunities for each student. The major area of decision-making in the assessment sub-component is *deciding what information to gather.*

This decision is an important one. Unless the information-gathering procedures are carefully chosen, students are likely to be overcome with information-giving and teachers burdened with more information than is useable. It is, therefore, important to strike a balance between information needed and concerns for student sensitivities about giving information. Generally, it is a good idea to collect only that information which you know you will use for specific purposes. To do this requires that a data-gathering plan be formulated which includes what data will be gathered throughout the instructional program. Ordinarily, the bulk of information will be obtained at the beginning of or prior to instruction. This is a good strategy, but subsequent data-gathering should not be ignored. That is, a plan should be formulated which includes regular data-gathering throughout an instructional program. Before explaining the reasons for planning regular data-gathering, let's take a brief look at some basic concepts associated with assessment.

Reliability. Reliability is a concept that can be appropriately applied to any data-gathering. This includes anecdotal information, self-reports, teacher-made tests, questionnaires, and standardized tests. Reliability refers to the confidence you can place in data. Some tests yield useable information on a consistent basis, while others do not. Therefore, it is important to choose procedures which are reliable. The basic procedure for establishing reliability is to seek alternate, independent observations of the same behavior. This is really just seeking collaborative data from a second or third source.

In assessment, reliability can be accounted for by looking for trends and supportive data in the information gathered. That is, independent support for major conclusions should be sought. If several sources disagree, then further assessment should be conducted in order to determine what the data actually indicate. The major implication for instructional designers is that no major decisions should be based on one piece or source of information. Several should be used to insure reliability.

Norm. A norm is essentially a standard pattern of scores derived from a large sample of individuals who have taken a test. The advantage of a norm is that it provides a benchmark against which individual scores can be compared. This gives an indication of how an individual ranks with all others who have taken the test.

It should be remembered, though, that test norms are statistical orderings of scores. As such, individual test scores are subject to some error. Thus, the real score could easily fall anywhere within a range of scores. This is an important point, since the range is frequently large. Thus, it is sometimes difficult to use norms without additional supportive data. This is true regardless of the reliability reported for the test.

Standardized Test. A standardized test is one for which norms have been developed and for which a basis of comparison is available. These tests, also called norm-referenced tests, are quite difficult to prepare. The tests are often used to estimate the relative amount of an attribute, aptitude, or characteristic possessed by an individual. For example, an individual who achieves high scores on an intelligence test is said to have a high IQ. A person who scores high on an anxiety test is said to be very anxious. Standardized tests are frequently used to measure aptitudes and, based on research results, can often be helpful in decision-making relative to manipulation of a range of instructional variables.

Validity. Validity refers to whether a test measures what it purports to measure. The validity of published instruments is ordinarily fairly well-established and discussed in test manuals. The validity of teacher-made assessment devices is not so well-established and should be questioned by the instructional developer when using this type of instrument.

Categories of Information

Let's turn our attention now to some information which will contribute to an understanding of students. The need for information in any of these categories varies, depending on several considerations. One of these is the length of time students will be involved in an instructional program. The longer the involvement, the more changes in students are likely to occur; and, therefore, more information is needed on a continuing basis. Another consideration is the type of learning desired. When students are entering into a novel learning experience, more data are needed than when they are embarking on familiar forms of learning. One must also consider the previous experience of students relative to the learning desired. When previous experience or prerequisites are required for successful entry into an instructional program, more information is needed than when no prerequisites are needed.

General Descriptive Information. The first category of information we will discuss is general descriptive information. All data of a general nature which can be utilized to make decisions on students are included in this category. Ordinarily, this will be information gathered from all students. The purpose for the data is to provide a general picture of incoming students to be served by the instructional program. Some of the data may be available from school records or other sources, while other information may need to be gathered from students directly.

There are several techniques which may be used to gather these descriptive data. These include teacher-made or specially designed instruments such as questionnaires, projective instruments, and standardized tests. A common practice for relatively long-term involvement, such as a full year, is to ask students to supply demographic data through a questionnaire. Generally, students are asked to supply information about their home situation, previous school activities, and personal preferences. Data of this type can lead to a general understanding of students. In addition, these data can point to specific areas where additional follow-up data may be needed.

Follow-Up Information. When general descriptive information is indicative of potential problems, then specific information needs to be gathered. For example, if a child indicates a dislike for school or a particular subject, a teacher should pursue this to identify how he or she might best confront the situation. Follow-up data can be gathered through a number of techniques. Most of these are relatively time-consuming, since the process is usually probing and exhaustive. Some techniques frequently employed are interviews, projective devices, standardized personality tests, and specially developed questionnaires.

A major issue here is determining whether follow-up data are needed. Some such data may be needed from every student, but most can be gathered informally. Formal follow-up procedures should be implemented when serious questions are raised in the teacher's mind relative to the student's potential for success in the instruction being designed.

Situation-Specific Information. The third general category of information we will discuss is situation-specific information. This includes information which may be important for a particular curriculum or content. For example, some specific health information is necessary for physical education classes. Such information is usually gathered specifically for the physical education class. Teachers, too, often want to get specific information they have found useful in the past. This may include information related to special concerns or interests of the teacher, or information about specific classroom procedures. For example, a teacher who is interested in moral development may wish to gather some data on the general level of moral development among a group or from individual students. Information which relates to any special features of the teacher's beliefs about how children learn would also fall under this category.

Situation-specific information may be gathered in any way which is appropriate and convenient. Techniques are available which may be modified to fit almost any purpose. It is important, however, to always keep in mind problems which may arise due to reliability.

Information-Gathering Techniques
There are many ways to gather information. The selection of

one technique or another is usually a matter of personal preference and a function of the kind of information to be gathered. In this section, we will briefly review some general considerations to keep in mind in developing and using several types of information-gathering techniques.

Observation. Probably the most frequently used method for acquiring decision-making information is observation. Observation can be a good or a poor information-gathering technique. The major problem with observation is—the observer. Human beings generally are poor observers. This is because there is a tendency to over- or under-estimate frequency of various behaviors. Obnoxious behaviors are often estimated to occur much more frequently than they actually do. This is especially true for students who are perceived as being "troublemakers" or problem students. Thus, reliability is a major problem with observational data. The careful teacher-observer must use extreme caution to insure that his or her observations are accurate. In general, the best way to establish reliability is to seek independent observations. If these match his or her observations, the teacher has some data supporting reliability.

There are two basic kinds of observation; formal and informal. Informal observation should never be used for direct instructional decision-making. This is not to say that informal observation is inappropriate. Informal observation has a definite purpose, which is to provide data for tentative hypotheses. These tentative hypotheses should then be validated with formal observation. An example of this process would be a teacher who noticed that a student took an extremely long time to solve written math problems. Several tentative hypotheses could be generated to account for this. Perhaps the student did not know how to apply principles learned in computation exercises. Another hypothesis may be that the student does not read well or could not understand the logic of the written problem. The point here is that informal observation should result in the identification of a probable explanation for an observation. This may be a problem, such as described above, or it may be the observation of a unique way the student learns. Such observations, however, should be confirmed for reliability with more formal procedures before any instructional decisions are made.

Formal observation is direct observation of a well-defined behavior. The behavior should be defined in behavioral terms so that it is clear and easily observable. When a behavior is well-defined, it should be observable with high reliability by two or more observers. Also, behavioral definitions should focus on behavior rather than feelings or impressions. For example, thinking is not an observable behavior, and neither is attitude, unless clearly specified. On the other hand, talking, time off task, and paying attention can be readily observed, if carefully defined. It is important to note here that social as well as academic behaviors can be behaviorally defined. Thus, students' behavioral responses to instruction as well as discipline-related behaviors can be defined and observed.

There are two basic types of formal observation. The first, frequency counting, is the tabulation of the number of times a behavior occurs. This type of observation is used for discrete or non-continuous behaviors which have a clear beginning and end. Number of problems completed, use of adjectives, and accuracy in completing projects are examples of non-continuous behaviors. Once well-defined, a non-continuous behavior is recorded by simply keeping a record of each time it is observed. This can be done by making tally marks on a sheet of paper or by carrying a counter. The second type of formal observation is called a time sample. In a time sample, the observer monitors the situation at specified time intervals (e.g., every ten seconds) and makes a notation if the defined behaviors have occurred during that time period. A time sample is used when the behaviors being observed are continuous or have no clear beginning or end. Sitting, working, paying attention, and cooperating are examples of continuous behaviors. Continuous behaviors must be defined in the same manner as discrete behaviors; that is, the definition must focus on behavior and be clear and observable.

Many teachers object to doing formal observation because they feel it is too time-consuming. Certainly it is true that a teacher who spent all of his or her time observing would get little *teaching* done. However, teachers should not overlook formal observation as a powerful technique for gathering assessment data. Particularly during planning, more attention can be given to observation in order to develop a clear and accurate picture of individuals who make up a group. Formal observation probably takes no longer than other well-planned and carried out data-gathering procedures. The idea supporting formal observation is to get reliable data for decision-making; the method used to establish the reliability of observations is not as important as the fact that the observations have been established as reliable.

Interview. Interviews are good ways for getting detailed information. The major advantage of an interview is that it allows the interviewer to pursue issues in depth as they come up. The major disadvantage is that interviews can be time-consuming compared to questionnaires and observation. Like most assessment procedures, interviews can be conducted well and yield good decision-making data, or they can be a virtual waste of time if not properly prepared. The objective of an interview is to gather information which will be useful for making decisions. To accomplish this, the interview must be focused on relevant issues and controlled by the interviewer. The following guidelines should be helpful in constructing an interview for gathering useful data.

First, the interview should be well-planned. This means a specific purpose or purposes for the interview should be developed and the interview should be structured around these purposes. The purpose for an interview can be drawn from formal or informal observation or other data collection procedures. It is a good idea to have these purposes well-specified to the point of preparing specific questions so that you will know what to ask.

Second, questions should be carefully chosen so that they will elicit the information sought. Generally, questions should be open-ended and not answerable with a simple yes or no or other one-word response. For example, "Do you like school?" is not a good question, whereas "Tell me what you like about school" is a better one.

Third, have the interview organized in order to avoid confusion. Don't skip from topic to topic, but ask all questions on one topic and then move to the next.

Fourth, maintain control of the interview. Don't allow the topic of conversation to be changed to irrelevant matters or controlled by the student. If the topic is changed, you should indicate to the student that, while you are interested in other matters and concerns, the purpose now is to learn about the topic of the interview. Finally, be pleasant and honest. Don't try to bully information or trick students.

Be sure to take advantage of the major value of an interview, that is, the opportunity to treat issues in depth as they are raised. Do not hesitate to ask follow-up questions when students are unclear or when you have an impression that additional information may be useful. By the same token, do not pursue a single issue unceasingly if it proves unproductive. Remember, the purpose is to gather information, not to validate preconceptions which you have developed. If you do run into a snag on a particular issue, it sometimes helps to go on to another subject and return to the problem area near the close of the interview.

Questionnaires. A questionnaire is essentially a series of questions posed to students. As with other assessment procedures, questionnaires must be carefully planned in order to elicit useful information. The questions included in a questionnaire must be carefully constructed. Also, the questionnaire should be arranged nicely so that it looks attractive and not imposing. This is not a difficult thing to do if you keep in mind that a questionnaire is not a good technique for gathering detailed information. Questionnaires are designed to gather relatively straightforward, factual information. Detail can be added later through interviews or other interaction. The following guidelines will be helpful in developing questionnaires.

First, make sure the questions are clear and have only one meaning. Questions which are simple and straightforward are the best. Also, always use simple language which is easily understood. Many times the way a question is asked can make the difference between completing a long and short questionnaire. For example, if you wanted to get some family background data, you might ask, "How many brothers do you have?" and "How many sisters do you have?" and "How old are your brothers and sisters?" A much simpler way to get these data would be to ask the students to "List the names and ages of your brothers and sisters." Always try to use as few questions as possible to get the most information.

Second, the way in which a questionnaire is organized can make a difference. Questions should be well-organized so that they can be easily read and answered. There are two basic organizations for questionnaires: free-response and forced-choice. A free-re-sponse item is one to which the respondent supplies the whole answer. For example,

Father's occupation ....

Hobbies ....

A forced-choice item contains several alternatives from which the respondent chooses the best or most descriptive. For example,

How much schooling has your father had?

...... Eight years or less

...... Nine to 11 years

...... High School Graduate

...... One to three years of College

...... College Graduate

...... Other

Forced-choice questions are easily tabulated but yield less specific information. Thus, more follow-up is often necessary. Forced-choice items also take up more space.

Summary
The basic purpose of assessment is to gather decision-making information in order to arrange the instructional environment to be responsive to student learning needs. To do this, the teacher must make decisions about the information to be gathered and how to amass the needed data. A primary concern, regardless of the procedure employed to gather data, is the reliability and validity of those data.

To acquire data, it is necessary to construct a plan for data-gathering. This should be considered a process which is continuous throughout the instructional program. The assessment plan should include a specification of what information is needed, how the information is to be acquired, and the timing of data-gathering. Decisions about what data are gathered rest on the teacher's personal beliefs and theories of learning, the instructional features to be manipulated, and the special needs of students and curricular requirements. The procedures to be employed are decisions of personal preference and convenience. Decisions regarding timing of assessment activities depend on such factors as length of the instructional program, student familiarity with the content, and novelty of the instructional procedures. Subsequent chapters will suggest specific assessment techniques which may be used to gather decision-making data.

Part III: Structuring Learning

5

Goals

Goals are relatively broad statements which describe the gap between intentions and assessment results. The intentions state the purposes of the instruction in a general way. Assessment data indicate where students stand relative to these intentions. Once data are gathered, goals must be gathered which specify what students must be able to do in order to meet the intentions. The purposes for developing goals are to (1) define what is to be included in the instruction, and (2) provide a structural framework for content and process analyses.

In this chapter, we will discuss the process of developing goals and placing them in a relational order or sequence. We will also discuss different kinds of goals. Upon completion of this chapter, you should be able to describe what a goal is and the purpose of goals in designing responsive instruction.

What Is a Goal?

Goals are defined as *descriptors of global competencies which define the purposes of instruction.*

Let's examine this definition for special meanings and implications. First, let's look at *descriptors of global competencies.* Goals are developed in terms of global rather than specific actions. When we think of education, ordinarily the end-product is considered in terms of general abilities, such as "understanding," "appreciation," "able to draw conclusions," and so forth. In other words, our purposes for education are ordinarily quite broad (i.e., "is able to repair an engine") rather than in terms of specifics (i.e., all the abilities that are required to be able to fix an engine). We operate at this global level because, first, it is the *real* end-product we seek. There is little point in teaching facts about the Great Depression if these facts do not fit into a more general framework of economic, political, and social "understanding." Thus, the facts or micro abilities have importance only if they are incorporated by the learner into a global competence which includes other components, such as knowledge, concepts, skills, etc. The second reason we think of education in these global terms is that it would be impossible to list always all the specifics involved in an educational program. In order to communicate effectively, we develop categories which, by general agreement, *include* the specifics.

Define the purposes of instruction is the second part of the definition. It may seem contradictory to use the word "define" in conjunction with "global competencies." However, a goal should pretty well define what the purpose of instruction is, in a recognizable and evaluatable way. That is to say, goals must not be generated in an off-the-cuff manner as the purposes of all instruction. For example, when "understanding" of something is a goal, one must be able to recognize this understanding when it is present and also recognize when it is not present. The ability to evaluate "understanding" is critical here. If a goal contains a global competency statement, such as understanding, and there is no notion of how to evaluate it, then the goal is meaningless. It will hardly serve the instructional designer in making future decisions.

The first decision, then, that must be made about goals is whether or not they are meaningful in a real sense. Reality here is a relative matter and will vary from goal to goal; however, at an absolute minimum, the reality should be reflected in the ability to answer a question such as "What do you mean when you say 'understand'?" Once you are able to do this, the goal will be amenable to further specification into subgoals and specific objectives. As a result, the content included in the goal can be analyzed into type of learning and learning conditions.

Goal development is a deductive process beginning with general outcomes and continuing with their breakdown into more specific components. Ordinarily, the learner will begin with specifics in order to develop the global competencies defined in the goals. It must be kept in mind at all times, however, that the goal is not only the accumulation of specifics but also the development of the global competency. By beginning the design process with the global competency and always keeping it as the primary purpose of instruction, learning of the global competencies is much more likely.

Goal Development

Decisions about goals must be as responsive to learner needs as any other instructional decision. In developing goals, assessment data must be utilized to determine what global competencies the individual or group of students must master in order to meet instructional intentions. This is basically a process of comparing intentions with student assessment data and writing goals to define the global competencies that students must demonstrate to indicate competency.

The relationship between intentions, assessment, and goals is straightforward. Intentions are developed to describe the boundaries of what will be excluded from the instruction; and assessment, in part, is the process of determining where students stand relative to these intentions. Goals are the descriptors of what will be *included* in the instruction.

To exemplify the goal-setting process, let's look at the goals for this book on responsive instruction. First, the intentions for the book are to: (1) describe responsive instruction, and (2) present the responsive instruction model and process. Thus, we are not exploring learning theories or educational philosophies, although both are important for the design of instruction. If development in these areas is needed, it must be sought elsewhere. With a text such as this one, formal assessment of specific groups is not possible, since it is intended to reach a broad audience of educators. However, it is assumed that most readers will not be familiar with the concept of responsive instruction, and, therefore, the goals for this material must include all the concepts and processes of responsive instruction.

Based on this analysis, the goals for this book are:

1. Understand the concept of responsive instruction.
2. Understand instructional decision-making.
3. Know the components of responsive instruction.
4. Understand how to make instructional decisions within each instructional component.
5. Be able to apply the responsive instruction model in designing an instructional program.
6. Regard responsive instruction as a practical and effective procedure for designing instruction.

As you can see, these goals are very broad, global competencies. Each is specific enough, however, to provide direction for future decisions regarding what should be included in succeeding chapters. Also, each is amenable to evaluation and represents a synthesis of more specific pieces of information, concepts, skills, and so forth. For example, we could evaluate the first goal, "understand the concept of responsive instruction," by examining a student's explanation of the concept for inclusion of critical concepts, such as the role of teacher decisions, the kinds of decisions teachers can make, the need for utilization of logic, assessment data and empirical results, etc. One who is able to do this well would be considered to "understand" responsive instruction.

Kinds of Goals

It is important not only to think about goals in terms of global competencies but also to differentiate kinds of goals. In discussing intentions, the need to consider many kinds of intent was stressed. These different intentions must be reflected in the goals. To facilitate this, it may be helpful to think about different kinds of goals. Before actually looking at some goal classes, be mindful that our use of "content" is not limited to a set or well-defined body of knowledge, such as math or history or language development. Content includes whatever is to be taught as stated in the goals. Thus, when we speak of content, we are not limiting this to specific concepts, information, etc., associated with a *single discipline*. Content, then, is not limited to traditional categories of academic subject matter but includes all learning outcomes.

Let's look at some classes of goals:

Knowledge goals are goals which specify the accumulation of knowledge, facts, concepts, etc., which are included in a discipline. Competence on knowledge goals is usually demonstrated through recall and application of knowledge.

Customary goals are goals which define outcomes ordinarily stressed by a school system either by custom or legal mandate. These goals are expected to be a part of all instructional efforts to some degree and may or may not be a major focus of instruction.

Affective goals are goals which are oriented toward developing attitudes or feelings about what is being taught. A goal such as a "love of learning" is an example of affective goals. Competence on affective goals is usually evaluated in terms of free-choice selection by students and non-required utilization of content.

Process goals are goals aimed at teaching ways of responding to situations, or thinking strategies. Examples of processes are problem-solving, decision-making, and scientific method. Competence is evaluated in terms of the application of the process rather than the correctness of a product.

The major reason for including some discussion on types or classes of goals is that instruction almost always is intended to include more than specific subject matter competence. If the instruction does include such goals, *they should be explicitly stated and included in the design of instruction.* Failure to do so may result in these goals being unmet, since they were not *planned* as part of the learning experience.

Organization of Goals

Logic is probably the best way to organize goals. When analyzing goals, it may be apparent that some goals should precede others. Other goals may not relate to each other so easily. Here the decision-maker must decide on a sequence on the basis of experience and/or preference, or perhaps leave the decision to students, if possible. Still other goals may be a logical part of all other goals and thus must be considered always in relation to all other goals. This is particularly true of affective goals and customary goals. Such goals are pervasive in the instructional program and must serve as decision guides to be considered when making all instructional decisions.

It is obvious that goals must be placed in some order; however, research provides us with little help in determining the "best" order. Gagne (1973) stated that "one can do little better than follow either common sense or Skinner's prescription that the content be arranged 'in a plausible developmental order.' If, in fact, such an order is not followed, there is an absence of evidence that this will make much difference" (p. 26). Thus, whatever order is chosen, it should make sense to the designer, at least. One major consideration in the ordering of goals is that the prerequisites for one goal should be preceded by goals which include those prerequisites. This, however, seems so obvious that it need not be dealt with any further.

What we do need to consider are two different levels of goal organization. The first is the order between goals; the second is the order within goals. Our focus will be on the use of logic to establish goal organization at both levels, though it seems that Gagne's statement may apply more to the former.

Once we have established goals, it may appear that we are not a great deal better off than before the goals were developed. We have a series of relatively general statements which do not easily lend themselves to further analysis in terms of instructional decisions. For example, if the goal specifies "understanding," we need to know what this is in order to make decisions about specific instructional events which will facilitate understanding; and, at the same time, we must be responsive to student needs. What is required for this to be possible is a refinement of the goals. To do so, we must attend to the order within each goal.

Statements of global competencies must be broken down into sub-competencies which are a part of the global competency. The result of this refining process is an outline of what is to be taught, organized in a logical fashion. For example, one of the goals for this book is "understand instructional decision-making." We can break down this goal into two subgoals, in the following manner:

Understand Instructional Decision-Making.
1. Understand the Systems Approach.
2. Understand the Decision-Making Process.

By doing so, we have further specified what we mean when we say "understand instructional decision-making." Our subgoals, however, still represent relatively global competencies which need additional refinement.

Understand Instructional Decision-Making.
1. Understand the Systems Approach.
    A. Understand the Form of Systems Analysis.
    B. Understand the Substance of Systems Analysis.
2. Understand the Decision-Making Process.
    A. Understand General Orientation.
    B. Understand Identification of Intended Outcomes.
    C. Understand the Generation of Alternatives.
    D. Understand Decision-Making.
    E. Understand Verification.

This process has several advantages. First, the content can be put into a logical order. Second, the content can be carefully thought out so that nothing is omitted at each level. Third, the teacher can become thoroughly immersed in the content. Fourth, the organization is available for careful scrutiny by others and for subsequent evaluation. Finally, the content is specified to the point where it is possible to subject it to an analysis of what students need to know in order to meet the goal and what the teacher needs to do to be responsive to student learning needs.

This process of goal refinement should continue until a point is reached where one can begin to specify relatively specific competencies which learners must acquire in order to begin the learning process of meeting first subgoals and then the major goals. The decision on where to stop must be based on the characteristics of the content, the learners to be involved, and the reasoned judgments of the instructional designer. The decision is clearly a relative one and will be idiosyncratic to specific instructional design situations.

Decision-Making

Decisions about goals include what the goals should be and how they should be organized. These decisions have a major impact on all the other instructional decisions which must be made in the design of instruction. The result of decisions about goals should be a series of well-organized goals and subgoals which define the purposes of the instruction.

There is no formula for determining the adequacy of these decisions. This is one area of instructional design where one must rely to a great extent on intuition, experience, and educational philosophy. However, all decisions should be developed in response to well-established intentions and assessment data in order to be responsive to student needs and situational demands. Reliance on these data will help insure that the goals will be appropriate and will serve the needs of the students involved.

Summary

Goal development is the process of working out statements of global competencies which define the content of instruction. Goals define the gap between intentions and the position of students relative to these intentions as indicated by assessment data. Goals must be organized into a network of statements which include goals and subgoals. The major decisions in this sub-component involve the development and structure of goals which are responsive to student learning needs. The decision process must be guided by experience, logic, and educational and instructional philosophies. The purpose of goals is to provide a structure of content which can be subjected to further structural analysis in order to identify specific competencies and learning events which will be responsive to student needs.

Reference

Gagne, R.M. Learning and Instructional Sequence. In F.N. Kerlinger (Ed.), *Review of Research in Education.* Itasca, Ill.: F.E. Peacock Publishers, Inc., 1973.

6

Content of Learning/Learning Processes

The next two sub-components of responsive instruction are content of learning and learning processes; both will be discussed in this chapter. Content of learning involves the analysis of goals and subgoals into separate components to determine the kind of competencies which are to be taught. Learning processes involve the further analysis of these content components in order to determine the specific competencies to be taught and the kinds of activities which will facilitate student learning. Both components require many teacher decisions which may be critical to student learning. The purposes of this chapter are to alert you to the need for these decisions and to present a methodology for making decisions. After completing this chapter, you should be able to analyze goals into content components, specify instructional elements, and relate these to learning processes.

Content of Learning

Let's begin with a definition of this sub-component and an analysis of this definition. *Content of learning is the process of analyzing goal statements into content components.* As indicated earlier, the term content signifies what students are to be taught. The identification of what is to be learned is by no means a simple matter and involves much more than designating a subject matter (i.e., chemistry or history). Teaching chemistry, for example, involves presentation of knowledge, concepts, processes, etc. When we look at what is being taught, we must specify precisely the content components which students must learn.

The first phrase of the definition we will look at is the *process of analyzing goal statements.* This process is tied directly to goals. All goals should be included in the analysis so that the content of instruction will be understood. The process is a two-step procedure beginning with analysis of the goals, using a recognized analytic procedure, and ending with analysis of these goals into requisite components. The actual process for goal analysis depends on teacher choice. We will look at three commonly used classification procedures for analyzing content. All are useful and serve essentially the same purpose. However, regardless of the procedure decided upon, a specific process should be employed in order to provide the specification necessary to conduct further analyses and establish learning objectives. The next phrase is *content components.* We refer to the needed prerequisite learning which must be mastered in order to meet the goals. These content components of learning define the kind of learning or learning outcomes which students must acquire in order to master the content.

We will review three different procedures for classifying learning outcomes into content components and then cover the process of identifying the content components of these outcomes.

Classification of learning outcomes. We will review procedures for classifying learning outcomes developed by Bloom and his associates (Bloom, Hastings, and Madaus, 1971), Gagne (1974a), and Landa (1976).

Probably the best known of all classifications of learning outcomes are the taxonomies of educational objectives: the *Taxonomy of Educational Objectives: The Classification of Educational Goals. Handbook 1. Cognitive Domain* (Bloom, 1956) and the *Taxonomy of Educational Objectives: The Classification of Educational Goals. Handbook 2. Affective Domain* (Krathwohl, Bloom, and Masia, 1964). In these taxonomies, a hierarchical structure is assumed. That is, they represent a continuum from simple to complex with each category including the objectives below it, but not those above it. Thus, if a goal is classified at a higher level in the taxonomy, it is necessary that students possess the levels of outcomes below it.

The following are the major categories, in hierarchical order, of the cognitive domain. Lower level outcomes appear first.

1. Knowledge—"involves recall of specifics and universals, the recall of methods and processes, or the recall of pattern, structure, or setting" (Bloom, Hastings, and Madaus, 1971, p. 271).
2. Comprehension—"represents the lowest level of understanding .... the individual knows what is being communicated and can make use of the material or idea ... without necessarily relating it to other material . . ." (Bloom, Hastings, and Madaus, 1971, p. 272).
3. Application—"The use of abstractions in particular and concrete situations" (Bloom, Hastings, and Madaus, 1971, p. 272).
4. Analysis—"The breakdown of a communication into its constituent elements or parts such that the relative hierarchy of ideas is made clear and/or relations between the ideas expressed are made explicit" (Bloom, Hastings, and Madaus, 1971, p. 272).
5. Synthesis—"The putting together of elements and parts so as to form a whole" (Bloom, Hastings, and Madaus, 1971, p. 272).
6. Evaluation—"Judgments about the value of material and methods for given purposes" (Bloom, Hastings, and Madaus, 1971, p. 273).

Bloom specified sub-categories under most major categories in the taxonomy on the cognitive domain. The use of these sub-categories may make classification easier and, if Bloom's approach is used, greater familiarity with this taxonomy is recommended. If the basic assumptions of Bloom's taxonomy are accepted, then it has some decided advantages. That is, if you agree that the outcomes Bloom identified are hierarchical and comprehensive relative to cognitive learning, then classification of goals facilitates the identification of necessary outcomes or content components which precede the attainment of the goal. For example, if a goal is classified as an analysis goal, then the instruction must include knowledge, comprehension, and application outcomes before the analysis level can be reached. Thus, the next step in content of learning is to identify what knowledge, comprehension, and application outcomes must be included in the instruction to prepare the student to meet the analysis goal.

This illustrates one of the critical elements in identifying content components. Once a goal or subgoal is classified, it must be analyzed in order to identify necessary prerequisites for meeting the goal. These prerequisites are identified in terms of the classes of outcomes which are prerequisite to the outcomes specified in the goal statement.

Krathwohl, Bloom, and Masia (1964) also developed a taxonomy for the affective domain. For the sake of brevity, we will list only the major categories of the domain. It should be pointed out, however, that this is one of the few attempts that has been made to deal with affective outcomes in a systematic manner. Therefore, when affective outcomes are sought as instructional goals, these categories may be quite helpful in designing instruction to achieve these goals.

1. Receiving (attending)
2. Responding
3. Valuing
4. Organization
5. Characterization by a Value or Value Complex

The second classification scheme we will review is that of Robert M. Gagne (1974a). Gagne includes five major categories, as follows, with sub-categories as indicated:

1. Verbal Information—"Knowing that" (Gagne, 1974a)
   a. Labels—attaching a label or name to an object or event.
   b. Facts—an expression of a relationship between two or more named objects or events.
   c. Bodies of Knowledge—"interconnected facts, such as those pertaining to periods of history or to categories of art, science, or literature . . ." (Gagne and Briggs, 1974, p. 60).
2. Intellectual Skills—"Knowing how" (Gagne, 1974a)
   a. Discrimination—distinguishing one object/symbol from another.

    b. Concrete Concepts—identifying an object property or object attribute (these properties or attributes may be pointed to).

    c. Defined Concepts—"demonstrate the 'meaning' of some particular class of objects, events, or relations" (Gagne and Briggs, 1974, p. 42).

    d. Rules—demonstrate a class of relationships among classes of objects and events.

    e. Higher-Order Rules—Problem-Solving—"invented" rules for the purpose of solving a practical problem or class of problems.

3. Cognitive Strategies—"An *internally organized* skill which governs the learner's own behavior" (Gagne and Briggs, 1974, p. 47).

4. Attitudes—"Complex states of the human organism which affect his behavior toward people, things, and events" (Gagne and Briggs, 1974, p. 61).

5. Motor Skills—"Learned capabilities that underlie performances whose outcomes are reflected in the rapidity, accuracy, force, or smoothness of bodily movement" (Gagne and Briggs, 1974, p. 66).

The structure of these learning classes is not strictly hierarchical. That is, the separate major categories tend to be independent. However, where sub-categories are included, these are meant to be hierarchical, with the first sub-category being the lowest level. It does appear, however, that verbal information is a prerequisite to all the other categories, particularly intellectual skills. The use of this classification procedure, if one accepts it, allows for identification of prerequisite learning, as does Bloom's. Gagne (Gagne, 1974a; Gagne and Briggs, 1974) also attached learning conditions to each of the major categories. These learning conditions define the substance of instructional events which must be present for learners to acquire the outcomes specified. This will be particularly helpful in the next phase of structuring decisions in the learning process component.

The third procedure for classifying goals into learning outcomes is based on the work of L.N. Landa (Landa, 1976). Landa's procedure is quite different from those of Bloom and Gagne and may have only limited applicability at this time. However, where applicable, Landa's ideas may serve the instructional design very well in analyzing outcomes. It is also possible that Landa's ideas may be useful in further analyzing and structuring content following an analysis according to either Bloom or Gagne.

Landa has worked extensively in the application of cybernetic principles to instructional design. A major element in this approach is to establish control over the learning process; this control requires:

(1) a precisely defined objective;
(2) an effective and precisely defined program of control;
(3) good feedback, i.e., consideration of changes taking place in the controlled system; and
(4) adaptive influences on the controlled system according to a decision based on consideration of the relation between the objectives and the present state of the controlled system (Landa, 1976, p. 37).

The controlled system in instruction is the student, and the controlling system is the instruction. Landa was obviously writing about an instructional program which would obtain maximum responsiveness to students as they learn.

Landa's approach to content structure is to divide learning outcomes into two broad categories: algorithmic learning and heuristic learning. The purpose is to establish control over the thought processes students use while learning. Landa places great emphasis on the use of the rules of logic in establishing such control. Algorithms are derived from logical statements in an "If . . . then" format, which describes the relation between two or more objects and attributes. In other words, algorithms are rules.

Landa identified two kinds of algorithms: identification algorithms and transformation algorithms. In both cases, in order for the learning to be algorithmic, three basic properties must be present:

1. Specificity—"indicates the fact that all actions of the user . . . are unambiguously determined by instructions (rules), and that these instructions are identically (or

uniformly) understandable and understood by all us-
ers . . ." (Landa, 1976, p. 108).

2. Generality—"means applicability of an algorithm to an entire (often infinite) set of problems belonging to a particular class" (Landa, 1976, p. 108).

3. Resultivity—"indicates that the algorithm is always direc-ted toward achieving the sought-after result, which the user, once he possesses the appropriate initial data, always achieves" (Landa, 1976, p. 108).

In essence, an algorithm is a rule for using a rule. That is, it specifies how a rule is to be used, and if used in the manner indicated in the algorithm, the result will always be correct.

Heuristics, on the other hand, do not possess the above properties. Of particular note is the absence of resultivity. That is, it is possible for two learners to come up with different solutions given the same information and problem. Landa (1976) defines heuristics "as specific rules of instruction governing actions and not . . . the actions themselves or any processes influencing the solution of a problem involving creativity" (p. 106). He further stated, "we will understand heuristics as meaning rules of heuristic activity, or as instructions on how to perform this activity." An example of a heuristic is the decision-making process described in Chapter 1. While a definite procedure is described for decision-making, it is clear that not everyone would generate the same decision. It is also impossible to predict which decision would be better, if both are reasonable.

Content Components. The next step in the analysis of the content of learning is to identify the necessary components of the content the learner will need to acquire in order to master the goal. In order to master an analysis level goal, for example, it is necessary for the learner to possess knowledge, comprehension, and application learning according to Bloom's taxonomy. The same procedure may be used with the Gagne schema. That is, given the particular goal in question, what content components must the learner acquire in order to be able to meet the goal?

This analysis into content components has three advantages. First, the designer becomes aware in a general way of the content that must be taught to enable learners to achieve. Second, it provides an operational framework for further analysis of the content into specific competencies. Third, the analysis provides a guide to sequencing content into a manageable order for the instructional design.

The process of identifying content components should be carried out for each goal. Once completed, these content components should be reviewed relative to intentions and assessment data in order to determine which specific content components should be included as a part of the instructional program. For example, if verbal information is a necessary content component, it must be decided if students do or do not already possess this information. The purpose here is to nail down the content components students do not possess. These then become the focus of the instruction. This decision is made on the basis of assessment data indicating past achievement relative to the intentions. It is also possible to require students to have already acquired specific levels of knowledge, rules, etc., as entry skills or readiness in order to be admitted to the instructional program.

Summary. Content of learning includes two basic processes. The first is analysis of goals into content outcomes according to a specific classification system. The purpose for this is to classify the goals into manageable outcomes. The second process is an analysis of these content outcomes into content components in order to identify the specific prerequisites students will need to learn in order to master the goals. Decisions in the former are based upon the chosen classification schema; we reviewed three such schema, but it is clearly possible to identify others or to originate a unique system. Decisions in the latter process are based on assessment data indicating which prerequisites students possess and which they need to learn. As a result of these analyses, the instructional designer has identified a series of outcomes and needed content components which must be included in the instruction. These content components may then be analyzed further into specific competencies and associated learning conditions in the next component, learning processes.

Learning Processes

The next sub-component is learning processes. The purposes here are (1) to specify the content component into specific competencies, and (2) to identify the necessary conditions which must be present to facilitate the learning of these competencies. We define learning processes as *the analysis of content into instructional elements.* The majority of decisions in this component are analytic in nature and rely heavily on the utilization of a systematic strategy as was employed in the analysis of content in the content of learning component.

We will begin by reviewing the definition. The first phrase we will look at is *the analysis of content.* This refers to the analysis accomplished in the content of learning component. This resulted in a list of general prerequisites which must be learned by students in order to meet the goals. That is, we now know students must acquire knowledge, comprehension, etc., or verbal information, discriminations, etc. We also have a relatively good idea of the content component prerequisites students have already mastered and those which must be mastered through the instruction. At this point, the content to be included in the instruction must be specified *into instructional elements.* That is, they must be cast into a form which is appropriate for learning. If knowledge is required, we must know what knowledge specifically must be learned. If rules are required, we must know which rules, etc. Thus, at this point, we are beginning to specify the substance of the content components. In addition, we need to identify the learning conditions which must be included in the instruction to promote this learning.

This sub-component is labeled learning processes because it consists of the specific elements and conditions the learner must process and interact with in order to master the goals. Decisions in this sub-component determine the form of the content students will interact with, the sequence of the content, and, to a large extent, the way in which the interaction will take place between student and content. There is, then, a direct impact from these decisions on the learning processes students employ to learn the content. If these decisions are responsive to learner needs, there is a greater likelihood that learning will be enhanced.

There are two major tasks in determining learning processes. The first is the identification of the specific instructional elements which make up the content components. The second is the identification of conditions necessary for the learning to take place. We will deal with each separately below.

Identification of Instructional Elements. Once it is clear that students must possess some knowledge, rules, comprehension, etc., it is necessary to identify the specifics to be learned. Each content component must be reviewed. For example, if the goal of instruction is to "understand the generation of alternatives" (this is actually a subgoal stated in the chapter on goals), we must first determine the content. In this case, the content is at the synthesis level, according to Bloom. The next step is to identify the content components, which are knowledge, comprehension, application, and analysis. At this point, we are ready to identify the specific instructional elements. Thus, we can ask, what knowledge is necessary? One piece of knowledge students will need is a definition of "alternative." Another is knowledge of steps in the decision-making process. This analysis should be continued until all the necessary knowledge that students will need has been determined. The same process should be conducted to determine the specific instructional elements of all other content components.

This process yields a content structure organized in a sequential manner. That is, the various elements students must learn are organized in a hierarchical structure which begins with the most basic elements and ascends to the most complex—each of the more basic elements being required for mastery of the more complex.

Exactly what specific instructional elements should be included is a matter of considerable concern. One process, suggested by Gagne (1974b), is task analysis. Gagne stated, "The purpose of task analysis . . . is to identify a number of *different classes* of learning outcomes—performances which require *different* learning conditions for their attainment" (p. 5). The technique of task analysis is to begin with the final human performance and ask the question, "What must the learner be able to do in order to learn this new element, given only instructions?" (White, 1974). The question is repeated for each newly identified element until the learner's entry level is reached. The resulting learning outcomes are the essential prerequisites for the specified goal.

Decisions about instructional elements must be based on the nature of the content (content components), learner readiness, and a thorough understanding of the subject matter. The process is essentially analytic and based on the logic of including or excluding specific instructional elements. The process is quite important, since these instructional elements represent what the learner must know or internalize in order to master the goal. The advantages of this analysis are fourfold. First, it is possible to specify to students what they are to learn. Second, the designer has the opportunity to key evaluation and remediation to the instructional elements. Third, it is possible to identify missing elements more easily when instructional problems occur. Fourth, the parameters of the content become familiar to the teacher in terms of content and structure.

Identification of Learning Conditions. The next step in the learning processes sub-component is to identify specific learning conditions which are necessary for students to learn the instructional elements. The idea of learning conditions has been most closely associated with Gagne (Gagne, 1974a, 1974b). Gagne (1974a) stated, "We must examine the specific events that facilitate learning for verbal information, for intellectual skills, for cognitive strategies, for attitudes, and for motor skills. We call these events the *conditions of learning*" (pp. 71-72). These conditions are essentially instructional events over which the teacher has control and which are obviously the result of specific teacher decisions. Gagne stressed the importance of conditions of learning because different conditions are necessary for different kinds of learning. The purpose of analyzing learning conditions is to attach specific learning conditions to the identified instructional elements. These conditions being the minimum necessary instructional features which must be present to facilitate effective learning.

We can turn to Gagne for guidance about these learning conditions, at least for the categories of learning which he defines.

Of course, if one is using the classification of Bloom or Landa, the explicit learning conditions may vary somewhat or be entirely different. Let's look at the learning conditions which Gagne (1974a) identifies as critical influencers of learning processes for each of his five categories.

For verbal information, the critical conditions are:
1. "Activating attention by variation in print or speech"
2. "Presenting a meaningful context (including imagery) for effective coding"

For intellectual skills, the critical conditions are:
1. "Stimulating the retrieval of previously learned component skills"
2. "Presenting verbal cues to the ordering of the combination of component skills"
3. "Scheduling occasions for spaced reviews"
4. "Using a variety of contexts to promote transfer"

For cognitive strategies, the critical conditions are:
1. "Verbal description of strategies"
2. "Providing frequent variety of occasions for the exercise of strategies, by posing novel problems to be solved"

For attitudes, the critical conditions are:
1. "Reminding the learner of success experiences following choice of particular action, alternatively, insuring identification with an admired 'human model' "
2. "Performing the chosen action; or observing feedback in the human model"
3. Giving feedback for successful performance; or observing feedback in the human model"

For motor skills, the critical conditions are:
1. "Presenting verbal or other guidance to cue the learning of the executive sub-routine"
2. "Arranging repeated practice"
3. "Furnishing feedback with immediacy and accuracy"

The identification of learning conditions associated with instructional elements has some obvious advantages for further instructional design. First, these conditions provide direction for decisions regarding the design of the situational context of the instruction. Second, they provide a framework for making decisions relative to how the instruction is to be delivered. Thus, by specifying these conditions, the teacher has a complete analysis of the content in terms of the kind of learning involved, the content components of the learning, the specific instructional elements, and learning conditions necessary to learn the content. This represents a complete analysis of the content and should also generate thorough understanding of what is to be taught.

Of course, additional decisions are needed relative to each learning condition, since they are identified in only a general way. For example, when "activate attention" is a condition, it must be decided how this is to be done. To a great extent, a thorough understanding of the content is required to make decisions about specific instructional actions which involve students in learning activities. These learning activities are the actions through which students acquire the abilities needed to meet goal statements. However, they are not the goals themselves.

Summary. The learning processes sub-component also consists of two procedures; identification of content components into instructional elements and identification of learning conditions associated with these elements. Decisions in both procedures are analytical in nature and should be based on a well-defined and organized structure. Three such structures were reviewed in the content of learning sub-component. The first procedure in the learning processes sub-component consists of identifying the specific instructional elements in order to identify the actual content which must be learned. The second procedure consists of identifying the learning conditions which must be present to facilitate the learning of the instructional elements. These analyses provide decision-making information which may be useful in making decisions on the design of the delivery of learning.

Summary

In order to summarize this chapter, it may be helpful to provide a complete picture of the content structuring activities to this point. To exemplify this process, we will look at an abbreviated analysis of a goal stated earlier for this book. The goal (actually a subgoal of a larger goal, understand instructional decision-making) we will analyze is "understand the generation of alternatives." In addition, we will look at this goal using the classification schemes of Bloom, Gagne, and Landa. You should be alert to several characteristics of this analysis. First, it is sequential, flowing from the goal to goal classification to analysis of content components to identification of instructional elements to identification of learning conditions. Second, it is judgmental with all decisions being open to disagreement. While there is little reason to believe that differences will greatly affect the quality of the instructional program, there is reason to believe that a failure to analyze content will result in lower quality instruction. Third, the analysis gives a very complete picture of the content to be taught. As a result, the teacher should have a thorough understanding of the content. Finally, you should note how these decisions can impact on all subsequent decisions. From this point on in the design process, the content will be a major factor to be considered along with student assessment data, logic, and empirical evidence in making instructional decisions.

The analysis of the goal, understand the generation of alternatives, is presented in Figure 6.1. The analysis is incomplete in that all the instructional elements in each content component are not included. However, some elements of every component are given as examples. Also, each classification includes the same content for comparison purposes.

As a result of the structuring activities to this point, we have a solid idea of what is to be taught and how the content is to be organized, and a general idea of what conditions must be present for students to learn effectively. We must complete one additional task to complete the structuring activities; this is to develop statements which can be used to inform students of the purposes of instruction. This is examined in the next chapter, Objectives.

References

Bloom, B.S. (Ed.) *Taxonomy of Educational Objectives: The*

Classification of Educational Goals. Handbook 1. Cognitive Domain. New York: Longman, Inc., 1956.

Bloom, B.S., Hastings, J.T., and Madaus, G.F. *Handbook on Formative and Summative Evaluation of Student Learning.* New York: McGraw-Hill Book Company, 1971.

Gagne, R.M. *Essentials of Learning for Instruction.* Hinsdale, Ill.: The Dryden Press, 1974a.

Gagne, R.M. Task Analysis–Its Relation to Content Analysis. Paper presented at the annual meeting of the American Educational Research Association, Chicago, Ill., 1974b.

Gagne, R.M., and Briggs, L.J. *Principles of Instructional Design.* New York: Holt, Rinehart, and Winston, 1974.

Krathwohl, D.R., Bloom, B.S., and Masia, B.B. *Taxonomy of Educational Objectives: The Classification of Educational Goals. Handbook 2. Affective Domain.* New York: Longman, Inc., 1964.

Landa, L.N. *Instructional Regulation and Control.* Englewood Cliffs, New Jersey: Educational Technology Publications, 1976.

White, R.T. The Validation of a Learning Hierarchy. *American Educational Research Journal,* 1974, *11*, 121-136.

Figure 6.1 A Partial Structural Analysis of One Goal by Three Different Classification Schemes

Goal Organization	Content of Learning		Learning Processes	
	Goal Classification (content outcomes)	Content Components (prerequisites to goal)	Instructional Elements	Learning Conditions
Understand Instructional Decision-Making				
2. Understand the Decision-Making Process				
c. Understand the Generation of Alternatives	Synthesis (Bloom)	Knowledge	Define alternative Recall specific steps in decision-making process	Make knowledge available
		Comprehension	Describe decision-making process in own words	Verbal description of process Opportunities to engage in process

(Continued on Next Page)

Figure 6.1 (Continued)

| | Content of Learning | | Learning Processes | |
Goal Organization	Goal Classification (content outcomes)	Content Components (prerequisites to goal)	Instructional Elements	Learning Conditions
		Application	Participate in brainstorming	Brainstorming situation
		Analysis	Describe relationship between the components of alternative generation	Model process
		Synthesis	Understand generation of alternatives	Present with problem situation
	Higher-order rule (Gagne)	Verbal information Label	State the definition of alternative	Activate attention Present in a meaningful context
		Intellectual skills Defined concept	Classify real and spurious alternatives	Stimulate recall of needed skills

(Continued on Next Page)

Figure 6.1 (Continued)

Content of Learning			Learning Processes	
Goal Organization	Goal Classification (content outcomes)	Content Components (prerequisites to goal)	Instructional Elements	Learning Conditions
				Provide examples of real and spurious alternatives
		Rule	Demonstrate a procedure for generating alternatives	Stimulate recall of needed skills
				Provide ample practice opportunities
		Higher-order rule	Generate alternatives using a process	Stimulate recall of needed skills and rules
				Present a novel problem

(Continued on Next Page)

Figure 6.1 (Continued)

| | Content of Learning | | Learning Processes | |
Goal Organization	Goal Classification (content outcomes)	Content Components (prerequisites to goal)	Instructional Elements	Learning Conditions
				Provide practice opportunities
	Heuristic (Landa)	Identification	Define "alternatives"	Cast into "if . . . then" format
		Algorithm		Present algorithm
		Heuristic	Demonstrate rules to govern behavior	Present a model of the process

7

Objectives

The last sub-component in the structuring learning component is objectives. Upon completion of this sub-component, the content should be well-structured so that both teacher and student know what has to be learned and what must be done to demonstrate learning. Objectives are relatively specific statements which communicate to students the expected behaviors or performances they will be required to engage in to indicate what they have learned. Objectives play a vital role in the design of instruction and may also be quite important in directly facilitating student learning. The purposes of this chapter are to acquaint you with the role of objectives in instructional design, to review some of the relevant research on objectives, and to provide guidance in making decisions which will result in objectives being responsive to student needs. When you have completed this chapter, you should be aware of the decisions required to develop good objectives.

Let's begin with a definition. *Objectives are relatively specific statements of what students should be able to do following an instructional session.* We use the term "relatively" in the phrase *relatively specific statements* in recognition of the difficulty in always precisely specifying outcomes. In fact, most verbal statements are subject to variations in interpretation. This is not to imply that objectives should not be specific. They should be as specific as possible. However, the important issue is that the objective be specific enough so that there is little probability of misunderstanding. This probability may vary from student to student and from student group to student group depending upon past experiences and aptitudes. Later, we will examine some of the many formulas which have been put forward for writing specific objectives. The essential requirement is that both teacher and student understand the objective.

The next phrase in the definition is *what students should be able to do*. The focus here is on student behavior. This is a shift away from the focus of previous structuring activities. That is, all the previous activities in the structuring learning component have focused on the content itself in terms of what must be known or learned in order to meet the goal. Objectives bridge the gap between the content and the student by transforming what must be learned into behavioral performances. This is obviously a necessary step, since the only way we have of determining if students have learned is to observe their performance. It is performances, specified in objectives, which reflect student learning. The decision on what performances to require is obviously critical. Performances must be carefully selected as valid indicators that students have learned what was intended in the lesson. Perhaps we should point out here that objectives do not specify what students must learn—they specify what students should be able to do as a result of their learning. McAshan (1977) stated that the real purpose of education rests in the learning outcomes (what students must learn); objectives are indicators or ways of measuring if these learning outcomes have been reached.

The next phrase is *following an instructional session*. This implies that objectives represent relatively small components of behavior which are the focus of specific lessons. In other words, objectives are statements of behavioral performances which are the intended outcomes of short instructional sequences rather than a whole course. The specification of objectives to be met following an instructional session is important because they provide students with some direction for specific lessons, and they provide a basis for formative evaluation. This approach recognizes the contribution each session makes to overall learning. The exact size or time included for an "instructional session" will vary depending upon the content taught and students involved. In some cases, objectives may be stated for each hour of instruction or each class meeting;

in other cases, objectives may be stated on a weekly basis or on some other unit of organization. The important issue here is to decide which organizational unit makes the most sense for the students and content involved. This unit then should be used as the focus for writing objectives.

In the remainder of this chapter, we will discuss the purposes or functions of objectives; review research on objectives; and look at issues associated with writing objectives.

Purposes of Objectives

Fortunately, there appears to be relatively wide agreement on why objectives should be written. While some authors (e.g., Clark, 1972) may list more, most authors present three purposes for objectives (Duchastel and Merrill, 1973; Gronlund, 1970; Hernandez, 1971; Kibler, Barker, and Miles, 1970; Mager, 1962; Plowman, 1971; and Vargas, 1972). Those who present a greater or lesser number of purposes tend to either compress or expand the apparently widely accepted three purposes. These three purposes are:

1. Objectives communicate to the learner (facilitate learning).
2. Objectives provide guidance for evaluation.
3. Objectives provide guidance for instructional development.

There is a widespread assumption among writers on behavioral objectives that the presence of behavioral objectives results in students learning either more easily or more efficiently, or both. The idea is that "To help a person learn something, let him know what he is expected to do" (Vargas, 1972, p. 5). We will review the research on this issue later. As you can see, the idea is basically a reasonable one.

The belief that objectives facilitate evaluation is also widespread. After all, if one clearly states what students are expected to do as a result of instruction, then it is a relatively easy matter to observe if the performance is acceptable. In other words, objectives provide for behavioral performance which can be evaluated. This, again, is a reasonable idea and makes sense conceptually.

The third purpose is also based on reason. That is, a teacher must know what students are expected to do in order to prepare appropriate instruction. As Mager (1975) stated, "If you don't know where you are going, it is difficult to select a suitable means for getting there. Instructors simply function in a fog of their own making unless they know what they want their students to accomplish as a result of instruction" (p. 5).

Research on Objectives

Relatively little research is available on the effect of objectives in facilitating evaluation or instruction. The major reason for this lack of research is probably that both of these functions are logical extensions of a way of thinking about instructional design. As a result, they are less amenable to empirical investigation. In fact, since evidence to the contrary is not available, we should have no difficulty in accepting objectives as useful, given that the logic is sound relative to these two purposes. The third purpose, the facilitation of learning, has received considerably more empirical attention.

It may also be helpful to look at the behavioral objectives movement in general. The popularity of behavioral objectives through the middle and late sixties gave rise to a spate of articles either extolling or denigrating behavioral objectives. The major point of contention usually was over the word "behavioral." A behavioral objective was ordinarily described as a very precise statement which specified learner behavior (an observable action), the conditions under which the behavior was to be performed, and the criteria of acceptability for the behavior. Proponents pointed out the values of focusing on observable behavior while opponents pointed out the triviality of most observable behaviors *vis-a-vis* the real purposes of education.

The interest in this issue has waned in recent years. Kapfer (1977a), in the first of a two-issue series on behavioral objectives in *Educational Technology,* noted, "There appear to be fewer how-to-do-it articles, fewer articles describing behavioral objectives in such-and-such school program, and fewer unalterably polarized positions regarding the positives and negatives of the behavioral approach. Perhaps everything that is useful concerning the fundamentals has already been said" (p. 5). In fact, it appears that increasing recognition of the multi-dimensional nature of instruction has generally resulted in less concern about objectives as an entity in themselves and more attention to the role of objectives as a part of the instructional process.

Kapfer (1977b) generated the following generalizations based on the articles included in the *Educational Technology* series (May and June, 1977):

1. Behavioral objectives represent one tool for systematic instructional design and validation.
2. Behavioral objectives represent a significant step toward a more scientific approach to teaching and learning.
3. Behavioral objectives may be written at a variety of levels of inclusiveness to serve the varying needs of educational decision-makers, planners, implementers, and learners.
4. Highly specific behavioral objectives may be made meaningful by relating them to some type of variously labeled broader goals.
5. Behavioral objectives techniques may be shaped to meet emerging educational needs (p. 6).

Thus, it is possible to conclude that current interest in objectives has taken a turn toward broader concerns more in line with current knowledge about instruction and learning.

Duchastel and Merrill (1973) reviewed research related to the effects of behavioral objectives on learning. Relative to immediate retention, the results of ten studies were inconclusive; the same was essentially true for delayed retention. That is, about half the studies produced results in favor of behavioral objectives and half produced no difference. Investigation of interactions of objectives with type of learning appeared to support no advantage for the use of objectives. Mixed results were reported relative to interactions with learner characteristics. A small number of studies (seven) were reported, and only three appeared related to each other. A tentative conclusion may be that objectives potentially may interact with student characteristics, since some interaction was found in each study. It is difficult, however, to state the nature of these interactions. The presence of objectives did appear to reduce learning time in the studies reported investigating this dimension.

From this review and other sources, it appears that behavioral objectives may not always facilitate learning, but neither do they depress learning. Teachers should be sensitive to differential reactions from students to objectives; when this occurs, alternative decisions should be considered relative to the objectives stated. In particular, problems may be encountered relative to specificity, student attention to the objective, clarity or student understanding of the objective, and/or student "use" of the objective to facilitate learning. Overall, the use of objectives of some sort appears justifiable and reasonable, since they serve useful purposes in the instructional process.

Writing Objectives: Some Formulas

As noted earlier, there are many books on writing objectives. These will not be duplicated here; however, the criteria proposed by three authors will be described. These procedures are neither recommended nor opposed; the decision is largely a matter of personal style. There are also others you may like listed in the Reference section. You may even wish to make up your own style. More will be said about actually writing objectives in the next section, covering decisions relative to objectives.

Mager (1962, 1975) wrote the most famous and most cited book on behavioral objectives, *Preparing Instructional Objectives.* This book is given much of the credit for the boom of behavioral objectives during the mid-sixties. Mager (1962) specified three criteria:

> First, identify the terminal behavior by name. . . . Second, try to define the desired behavior further by describing the important conditions under which the behavior will occur. Third, specify the criteria of acceptable performance by describing how well the learner must perform to be considered acceptable (p. 12).

The following is one example Mager (1962) gave of a good objective:

> The student must be able to reply in grammatically correct French to 95 percent of the French questions that are put to him during an examination (p. 50).

Vargas (1972) included the following characteristics or requirements for behavioral objectives:

1. They refer to the student's behavior.
2. They specify observable behaviors.
3. They state a level of criterion of acceptable performance.
4. They do not contain unnecessary words (p. 59).

Vargas' book is rich in examples on how to write objectives at all levels of Bloom's cognitive taxonomy. The following example was included by Vargas to indicate "alternatives" to knowledge level objectives. For the knowledge objective, "To define 'compound' as 'a pure substance that is composed of two or more elements and whose composition is constant,' " Vargas presented the following alternatives:

Taxonomic Category	*Alternative Skills*	*Examples*
Comprehension	1. To tell in your own words what the term means.	1. To tell in your own words what a "compound" is.
Comprehension	2. To identify instances and non-instances of the concept (using ones not covered in class).	2. To tell which of several substances are compounds.
Comprehension	3. To give original examples of the concept and non-instances of it (any "application" of concept to concrete examples is "comprehension").	3. To name three compounds (other than ones used in class or readings) and three substances that are not compounds.
Synthesis	4. To create a product using the concept.	4. To create a compound (other than ones known to the student) and demonstrate that it is a compound.

Gagne and Briggs (1974) also have presented a set of criteria for good objectives; they stated:

> They (objectives) must first, describe the action that the student is taking. Obviously, too, an objective must describe the situation in which that action takes place. Something must usually be said about the limits within which the performance of the student will be expected to occur. And, most important of all, the objective must indicate what kind of human performance is involved. This means they must describe what kind of human capability is to be inferred from the performance that is under observation (p. 79).

This essentially translates into five components: action, object, situation, tools and other constraints, and capability to be learned. Gagne and Briggs went on to list a set of verbs which correspond to the capabilities in their taxonomies as follows:

Capability	*Verb*
Intellectual Skills	
Discrimination	Discriminates
Concrete Concept	Identifies
Defined Concept	Classifies
Rule	Demonstrates
Higher-Order Rule	Generates
Cognitive Strategy	Originates
Information	States
Motor Skill	Executes
Attitude	Chooses

These nine verbs, then, can be used to describe all learned capabilities in objectives.

Each of these authors stresses clarity and accuracy. That is, the terminal performance must be clearly stated so that students understand what end-performance is expected. The accuracy of this performance is also important. That is, the performance must be a valid indicator of what students are intended to learn. The content to be learned, as well as the subject matter, must be reflected in the objective. Knowing that an objective has five components according to Gagne and Briggs and stating these represents one kind of learning. Generating objectives which include these five components is a different kind of learning. The legitimacy of either is not in question; both are important. The concern is to be certain that the objective specifies a performance which is indicative of what is taught.

Writing Objectives: Some Decision Guidelines

In responsive instruction, objectives serve the same purposes ordinarily attributed to them: facilitate evaluation, communicate to students, and provide some direction for instruction. We will look at each of these purposes separately and will need to consider all three simultaneously when actually writing objectives.

First, objectives facilitate evaluation by providing a criterion of performance. As indicated earlier, this performance becomes the focus of evaluation activities. Performances which cannot be evaluated should not be included in objectives. It is critical that the performance genuinely reflects the learning described in the content. For example, if the content specifies rule learning, a performance, such as "listing," will not be a valid indicator of rule learning. Thus, it is very possible that the teacher will not know if students have learned as intended. When writing objectives, it is important to be aware of the content of learning as well as specific terminal performances.

Second, objectives communicate to students by identifying expectations. These expectations may provide students with a learning set or a purpose which allows them to focus and organize their own learning. Certainly, such an effort would vary from student to student. However, knowledge of intended outcomes will probably be helpful to most students and hinder few, if any. Letting students know terminal outcomes at the start of a lesson creates an opportunity to organize the class for students. That is, objectives can be presented; then the learning needed to meet the objectives can be described; then the activities (strategies) which will be available can be noted. As a result, students will have an explicit overview of the class or instructional session and perhaps be able to take advantage of learning-to-learn from this routine. Even if these advantages of communication are considered questionable, communication of outcomes to students seems reasonable just to let students (parents and others) know what they are paying for.

Third, objectives provide direction for instruction as an organizing structure for individual lessons or instructional segments. Once objectives have been generated from the content structure developed to this point, it is possible to begin breaking groups of objectives into clusters which will serve as objectives for a single lesson. The nature of the terminal performance will also affect decisions in other components, such as time, space, grouping, and evaluation.

Let's look at the process of writing objectives. This involves the coordinated consideration of three sources of information from the structure of learning, student assessment data, logic, and relevant empirical information. The writing of objectives requires relatively complex decisions in order to make objectives responsive to student needs. We should point out here, however, that to the extent that previous decisions on structuring learning have been responsive to student needs, the less specific consideration of student needs will be necessary in writing objectives. This is the case, since, as we shall see, objectives are drawn directly from previous structuring activities.

One goal in writing objectives is to translate the content into statements of terminal performance which will be indicators of student learning. To do this, the objectives must be based on the goals, content components, and instructional elements of the instruction. Decisions here must begin with the structure which has been developed with these three factors. The process is analytical and may be best accomplished in the following order.

First, examine the instructional element and ask the question, "Should there be one or more objectives for this element?" Alternatively, it may be that two or more instructional elements should be included in a single objective. Second, consider what kind of terminal performance would reflect acquisition of the instructional element. A decision here will be based on the instructional element itself as well as the content component in which it is included. Third, consider what criteria would be appropriate to include in the objectives. The decision on criteria rests to a large extent on the content component and the instructional element involved in the objective. The purpose of including criteria is to inform students on how their performance will be judged. In some cases, the criterion may be very specific, such as "identify *three* purposes for objectives." In other cases, the criterion may be more general, such as "generate a rationale for using objectives based on *an established philosophy of instruction.*" Criteria are stated in order to inform students of how their performances will be judged, not to avoid the responsibility of making judgments about performances.

Finally, the objective should be reviewed in order to determine if any further specification is needed. Since our intent is to inform students, the objective should be specific enough to assure that students are reasonably well-informed about what is expected. Remember that the performances specified in objectives are indicators of student learning. A single objective represents one of many possible performances which could conceivably provide such a demonstration. When students have problems meeting an objective or several objectives, the problem may lie in the performance specified or in the learning program designed to help students meet the objective. The relative importance of a single objective for any lesson may be quite small, so that failure to achieve one objective may be a matter of little concern where many objectives are involved. It is also possible to offer several alternative objectives through which essentially the same learning may be demonstrated with different performances.

The final step in the development of objectives is to organize the objectives into lesson size groups. This is a highly judgmental decision, which rests on teacher experience and learner abilities. It is relatively safe to assume that higher-ability students will be able to handle more objectives per unit of time. It also appears that students will be able to handle more objectives as they get deeper into the instructional program. Certainly, these decisions will vary in degree of success in that there may be too many, or too few, objectives. However, this is essentially a matter of adjusting the content to fit into a series of "logical breaks" or content units. The only guidance which can be used in making such decisions is to review the content structure looking for relatively whole units or closely related instructional elements. This decision, of course, also depends on the kind of objectives one chooses to write. A single objective, for example, may subsume many content elements or only one. This appears to be largely a matter of the style of the teacher and the way in which he or she prefers to work.

Summary

Objectives are statements of terminal performances which serve as indicators of student learning. Objectives serve three purposes in the design and delivery of instruction; facilitating learning, evaluation, and instruction. In writing objectives, the focus of design activities shifts from content to learner performance. This change in orientation is necessary in order to stimulate active learner involvement and to provide opportunities for demonstrations of learning. There are many ways to write objectives, the most frequently written about being behavioral objectives. There appear to be no advantages of one specific style of objective over another, so the format of the objective is largely a matter of teacher style. However, regardless of the style selected, the objective should clearly communicate to students and should be a valid indicator of student learning.

References

Clark, D.C. *Using Instructional Objectives in Teaching.* Glenview, Ill.: Scott, Foresman and Company, 1972.

Duchastel, P.C., and Merrill, P.F. The Effects of Behavioral Objectives on Learning: A Review of Empirical Studies. *Review of Educational Research,* 1973, *43,* 53-69.

Gagne, R.M., and Briggs, L.J. *Principles of Instructional Design.* New York: Holt, Rinehart, and Winston, Inc., 1974.

Gronlund, N.E. *Stating Behavioral Objectives for Classroom Instruction.* Toronto, Canada: The Macmillan Company, 1970.

Hernandez, D.E. *Writing Behavioral Objectives.* New York: Barnes and Noble, Inc., 1971.

Kapfer, M.B. Behavioral Objectives: The Position of the Pendulum—Introduction to Part One. *Educational Technology,* 1977a, *17*(5), 5-6.

Kapfer, M.B. Behavioral Objectives: The Position of the Pendulum—Introduction to Part Two. *Educational Technology,* 1977b, *1 7*(6), 5-6.

Kibler, R.J., Barker, L.L., and Miles, D.T. *Behavioral Objectives and Instruction.* Boston: Allyn and Bacon, Inc., 1970.

Mager, R.F. *Preparing Instructional Objectives.* Belmont, Calif.: Fearon Publishers, Inc., 1962.

Mager, R.F. *Preparing Instructional Objectives, Second Edition.* Belmont, Calif.: Fearon Publishers, Inc., 1975.

McAshan, H.H. Behavioral Objectives: The History and the Promise. *Educational Technology,* 1977, *1 7*(5), 36-44.

Plowman, P.D. *Behavioral Objectives.* Chicago: SRA, 1971.

Vargas, J.S. *Writing Worthwhile Behavioral Objectives.* New York: Harper and Row, 1972.

Part IV: Delivering Learning

8

Time

There are two sub-components of the responsive instruction model which relate to time: time to complete objectives and time to deliver objectives. Since the two are related, they will both be dealt with in this chapter. Before beginning with either specific sub-component, however, we will examine some general considerations associated with time and instructional decisions. It would seem that the consideration of time in instruction is relatively straightforward. Unfortunately, this is not the case, and there is a good deal of controversy currently about the role of time in instruction. We will begin by articulating the major dimensions of this controversy, particularly as these issues relate to decision-making.

The basic issue is whether students learn more when given additional time. This is not a new issue historically but has gained a good deal of attention through the work of Carroll (1963) and Bloom (see Bloom, Hastings, and Madaus, 1971). Carroll, in his model of school learning, included rate of learning as a major factor differentiating those who learn from those who do not. If you consider the normal way in which education is delivered, this appears to be a sensible postulate. That is, students are placed in a time-bound educational program; whether this is a course or a grade level, students are given a specific time frame in which a relatively set amount of learning must be mastered. If the learning is not mastered, then students are given evaluations of learning which reflect the reduced amount of learning required. This may range from almost all (indicated, perhaps, by a grade of B) to not nearly enough (indicated by an F).

Carroll's idea, and Bloom's also, is that the time constraint places an artificial limitation on learning. If given sufficient time, perhaps all or almost all students could achieve mastery. Thus, by eliminating time constraints, all students could achieve learning to mastery. It is a sensible idea that makes mastery learning a realistic possibility by taking the relatively simple step of allowing students more time to learn. Bloom (1971) articulated the problem for mastery learning as "to find ways of reducing the learning time [which] slower students require so that the task will not be prohibitively long and difficult for them" (p. 51).

Clearly, time is seen by Carroll and Bloom as a critical dimension. There are, however, a number of problems associated with variation of time. One major problem is determining how to set the amount of time a student will need. While giving several suggestions on how to establish learning rates, Carroll (1971) stated he knew of no research which reliably indicated how to establish or predict learning rates. There is a further complication associated with the measurement of learning rates. Learning rates are likely to be very idiosyncratic, varying from subject to subject for the same student. The greater problem, however, is in the measurement of learning rate. Measurement of rate requires careful monitoring of student progress during learning. This could be quite cumbersome in ordinary classroom settings. There is also the possibility of a good deal of error due to uncontrollable student factors and problems with measurement procedures which necessitate controlled observations.

Conceptualized most simply, learning rate could be considered the amount of time it takes a student to learn a set amount of material. However, there are a number of factors which could affect learning rates measured in this way. Motivation is one of the most obvious; given equal ability, a highly motivated student would probably learn faster than an unmotivated student. And motivation is likely not to be constant with any single student. A second problem arises in determining what the standard amount of learning for setting the learning rate should be. Content obviously varies in both complexity and interest value. Thus, not only are different students likely to respond at different rates, but also the same student is likely to respond at different rates as the content changes.

Two other issues must be discussed briefly. First, the amount of time it takes a student to learn, in addition to the factors already mentioned, is also a function of the quality of the instructional program. Here, quality refers to two dimensions, the "goodness" of the program itself and how well the program matches student learning needs. If students are given poor instruction, then it is probable that their learning rates will be slower than if they receive good instruction. In a similar vein, when instruction is matched to student learning style, students are likely to learn faster. This is an idea consistent with both Bloom and Carroll. That is, to be most efficient, instructional strategies must be matched to student learning aptitudes.

The second issue which we need to address concerns variations in learning rate depending on the type of learning required. Cronbach and Snow (1977) stated that a single rate measure was misleading. This is because at any given time the learner is probably acquiring several kinds of learning. For example, a student sitting in a chemistry class may be concurrently learning chemistry concepts and attitudes about chemistry. If learning rate were measured, each type of learning would probably have a different rate. Since other learning is probably occurring also (i.e., concept application, terminology, visual recognition, etc.), a very large number of learning rates could be generated; consequently, the concept of learning rate begins to lose meaning.

Cronbach and Snow (1977) have proposed learning "levels" as a more appropriate measure of learning relative to time. They defined level as a measure which "describes degree of mastery or proficiency after some specified amount of training" (p. 113). With the level scores, it is not necessary to set upper and lower limit scores as with the rate measure. That is, when rates are established, "The first standard must be set somewhere above the score of the poorest performer on the first trial. The high standard must be low enough to be reached by every *S* during the course of the experiment" (p. 115). The rate of learning, then, reflects how long it takes a student to achieve the high standard. The rate is obviously confounded by factors such as prior knowledge and motivation. Level scores reflect the amount (percentage) of learning a student achieves given a specific amount of training. Such training could be defined in terms of time, amount of content, or other appropriate dimensions.

Rate or learning speed clearly presents a number of problems for both teachers and researchers. Perhaps the ultimate question is whether consideration of rate really makes any difference. From a theoretical perspective, this may be the case. Cronbach and Snow (1977) make a convincing argument that learning rate is accurately predicted by aptitude scores and general intelligence scores. That is, students who score well on standardized aptitude and intelligence tests learn more quickly than those who do not score well. This trend appears to hold up regardless of age or content.

To this point, we have considered one time-related component, time to complete objectives, or learning rate. Our discussion has centered on several issues associated with rate of learning which complicate instructional decisions. We need to turn our attention to more practical concerns about rate of learning and instructional decision-making. However, before we do this, we will take a brief look at the other time component, time to deliver objectives, or pace.

Time to deliver objectives is a somewhat mysterious component. While it is clear that instruction can be paced differently, it is unclear what bases are used to vary instructional pace. For example, Barr (1975) asked teachers how they pace their instruction and found that teachers "seemed confused by questions on pacing" (p. 491). Teachers were unable to specify what led them to move faster or slower. Dahloff (1971) presented a hypothesis that teachers pace by gearing instruction to children falling between the tenth and twenty-fifth percentiles in the group. When children in this group appear to understand, then teachers move on to the next topic.

Available evidence seems to indicate that high-ability students can handle faster paced instruction, a finding which is hardly surprising. However, this must be considered a general rule-of-thumb rather than an absolute. Even brighter students do better with slower paced instruction in some instructional situations. The converse is not always true. That is, slowing the pace of instruction does not always improve achievement of lower aptitude students. This appears to indicate that lower aptitude students require more attention to instructional variables in order to increase achievement.

We will introduce a new concept associated with pace here; this is the notion of instructional efficiency. Instructional efficiency refers to the amount of time required for learning to take place. In very efficient instruction, students would learn a great deal in a short amount of time, while inefficient instruction would involve students for longer periods of time to learn smaller amounts. Efficient instruction is a goal for teachers. Establishing an efficiency rating requires that a set amount of learning be defined. Then one measures the time it takes students to reach a criterion level. One way to increase efficiency is to increase the pace of instruction. However, if increasing pace means that some students do not reach the criterion level, then effectiveness is sacrificed for efficiency. There are alternatives to regulating pace to increase efficiency; one of these is to utilize different instructional strategies. Strategies which coincide with student learning styles are likely to yield more efficiency than strategies which do not coincide with students' needs.

Efficiency of instruction is an important concept, since teachers must make decisions relative to how much efficiency they wish to achieve. In general, instruction with high aptitude students is likely to be more efficient than instruction with low aptitude students. Just altering pace with lower aptitude students does not automatically increase achievement. These students generally need a number of instructional variables specifically arranged to meet their learning needs in order to achieve. Even with several variables carefully arranged, instruction may not be as efficient as with high aptitude students. Therefore, in general, teachers should expect lower aptitude students to need more time to complete objectives as well as longer periods for delivery of objectives (pacing).

Practical Considerations in
Making Decisions About
Time and Learning

It is relatively clear by now that making decisions regarding both the rate at which students learn and the pacing of instruction is complex. We will try to provide some perspective for making these decisions within the context of responsive instruction.

Based on our previous discussions of responsive instruction, it follows that the pace of instruction should correspond to students' individual learning rates. That is, instruction should be designed in a way that is responsive to students' learning rates. Also, the pace of instruction should be such that maximum efficiency is reached for each student. The problem is in the doing, because these decisions are important, yet difficult to make.

You have undoubtedly noticed by now that the terminology used with responsive instruction is different from that used in the preceding discussion. Time to deliver objectives is used instead of pace and time to complete objectives is substituted for learning rate. For both components, the focus is on the objectives of instruction. Referencing these decisions to objectives provides a more solid basis for measurement and decision-making than what is ordinarily associated with either pace or rate. That is, the objective is the focus of decisions relative to learning rate and instructional pace.

Time to Complete Objectives. From a common-sense perspective, it seems reasonable to conclude that if students do not have sufficient time to learn, they may learn if given additional time. In fact, there is some evidence to support this. Bloom (1974) reported that "learners differ by a ratio of about 5:1 in their learning rates. That is, the slowest five percent of the learners take about five times as much time to reach the criterion as do the fastest five percent of the learners" (p. 684). Now, Bloom is speaking here of a comparison between the five percent at the top and the bottom of a normal or bell-shaped curve. It would be unusual to have such a spread of ability in every class. In any event, when the objective is used as a point of reference for time to learn decisions, the teacher has a relatively stable basis of comparison. Thus, it is possible to determine the relative amounts of time different students will require to meet learning criteria by measuring the time it takes them to complete objectives.

There are a number of practical ways to do this. One is to project the amount of time students will need based on their past performance. Students can keep a time-to-criterion record of their own performance, which can be used to make subsequent projections. One caution must be mentioned here. Students generally achieve to criterion more quickly on subsequent units when instructional units are sequenced. Bloom (1974) suggested that the ratio of fastest to slowest decreases to "about 3:1 or less" as students gain experience with an instructional program.

Time to complete objectives will probably decrease as students become more familiar with content and instructional procedures. However, this is predicated upon student motivation remaining relatively constant. Also, it is necessary for students to receive additional help when mastery is not achieved. Such help must be more than just repeating what they have done previously. That is, they must have remedial instruction qualitatively and quantitatively different from the original instruction.

It appears that initial estimates of time needed to master objectives may be based on two sources of information. First, aptitude tests may be used which relate to the instruction involved. Higher aptitude students are likely to need less time than lower aptitude students. By looking at composite scores for a group, a general idea of the amount of time the group will need can be estimated. If the group composite score is close to the norm, then an average time sequence can be planned. One also needs to examine the variability of scores in a group. If there is a great deal of variability, then the component time to complete objectives may require many individual decisions. On the other hand, if variability is low, this component may not be so critical for specific decisions.

Second, student past achievement can be a good indicator of time needed to complete objectives. High-ability students, as indicated by past achievement records, can generally be expected to need less time, and vice versa. Again, student achievement can be grouped for classes to give a general picture of ability for decision-making. As with aptitude, the range of achievement should be considered. Where the range is great, more attention would need to be given to allowing time variations.

Time to Deliver Objectives. The most pertinent research relative to time to deliver objectives appears to be found in studies on the amount of time students are in actual contact with content. This is also called time on task and academic engaged time. Rosenshine (1978) summed up a review of this research by saying "what is not taught and attended to in academic areas is not learned" (p. 6). The point here is that the amount of time scheduled is not as important as *the amount of time students are actually engaged in productive academic activity.* The actual engagement may be much more important than the speed at which the content is presented. Thus, students in a highly structured class for 30 minutes may be expected to have higher achievement than a class which is more loosely structured for 45 or 50 minutes, if class structure relates to content engagement.

Time to deliver objectives is referenced to the objective and thus provides a practical way to measure pace. Assuming that across time, the relative amount of time to deliver objectives will be roughly the same for each objective, a teacher can measure pace fairly adequately. Indices of incorrect pacing would be student boredom if too slow, or confusion, if too fast.

Barr (1974) noted that differential pacing was the most common technique used by teachers to individualize reading instruction. However, as noted earlier, teachers appear to do this instinctively and are unable to articulate a rationale for variations in pace. It also appears that alterations in pace do little to solve learning problems. That is, while faster pacing for brighter students may produce more achievement, slowing the pace alone for less able students does not improve learning. A study by Roechs (1978) indicated that teachers "were overzealous in their efforts as they utilized available instructional time better for low and high achieving students than for middle achieving students" (p. 21). It may be, then, that the "average" student is ordinarily expected to follow the pace set for either the very able or very poor student.

Explicit decisions on time to deliver objectives are difficult, and one must rely on the standard indicators, such as aptitude and prior achievement. More accurate decisions may be possible once instruction is begun and students have an opportunity to react. A general rule for time needed is to proceed as quickly as seems reasonable and moderate based on student achievement. Whatever time is made available, however, the major criterion for achievement appears to be how well the time available is utilized. When students are attending and engaged, then the time is fruitful and yields higher achievement.

Sources of Decision Information

1. *Aptitude measures.* These should be related directly to the instruction being designed. If standardized measures are unavailable, consideration of aptitude is probably risky.

2. *Achievement records.* These are probably the best source for time-related decisions. These records are ordinarily available and, unless highly variable, should give a relatively accurate picture of student potential.

3. *Student questionnaires.* Students may be questioned on their opinion of whether they are fast or slow learners. They may also be asked if school is usually too "fast" or "slow" for them. Such questions would be particularly appropriate when a new course is being designed, or there is a great deal of variability in student achievement and/or aptitude.

4. *Content reviews.* A good source for decisions on time to deliver objectives is to consider the amount of content delivered in comparable courses. This approach clearly has drawbacks, since comparable courses may be inappropriately timed and the content may not really be comparable. However, if several courses are considered, it is possible to get some rough estimates of the time students will need.

Summary

Two specific decision sub-components were reviewed relative to time and instruction: time to complete objectives and time to deliver objectives. These were related to research on learning rate and instructional pace, respectively. Learning rate is difficult to measure and a function of many student variables. Rate should probably be related directly to the achievement of individual objectives in order to have a relevant measure of rate. Decisions on learning rate or time made available for students to complete objectives should be based on student characteristics, particularly the students' past records of achievement. Time to deliver objectives should also be referenced to objectives to develop a standard for pacing instruction. These decisions should also be based on student characteristics and learning needs as reflected in student aptitudes and past achievement. Decisions about time in making instruction responsive to students should be made with the realization that (a) more able students will probably need less time, and (b) adjustments in both rate and pace estimates are likely to be necessary.

References

Barr, R.C. Instructional Pace Differences and Their Effect on Reading Acquisition. *Reading Research Quarterly,* 1974, *9,* 526-554.

Barr, R.C. How Children Are Taught to Read: Grouping and Pacing. *School Review,* 1975, *83,* 479-498.

Bloom, B.S. Mastery Learning. In J.H. Block (Ed.), *Mastery Learning.* New York: Holt, Rinehart, and Winston, 1971.

Bloom, B.S. Time and Learning. *American Psychologist,* 1974, *29,* 682-688.

Bloom, B.S., Hastings, J.T., and Madaus, G.F. *Handbook on Formative and Summative Evaluation of Student Learning.* New York: McGraw-Hill Book Company, 1971.

Carroll, J.B. A Model of School Learning. *Teachers College Record,* 1963, *64,* 723-733.

Carroll, J.B. Problems of Measurement Related to the Concept of Learning for Mastery. In J.H. Block (Ed.), *Mastery Learning.* New York: Holt, Rinehart, and Winston, 1971.

Cronbach, L.J., and Snow, R.E. *Aptitudes and Instructional Methods.* New York: Irvington Publishers, Inc., 1977.

Dahloff, U.S. *Ability Grouping, Content Validity, and Curriculum Process Analysis.* New York: Teachers College Press, 1971.

Roechs, A.C. Instructional Cost and Utilization of Classroom Time for Fifth Grade Students. Paper presented at the annual meeting of the American Educational Research Association, Toronto, 1978.

Rosenshine, B.V. Academic Engaged Time, Content Covered, and Direct Instruction. Paper presented at the meeting of the American Association of Colleges of Teacher Education, Chicago, 1978.

9

Message Channel

Message channel concerns the characteristics of the way in which the instructional message is communicated. Human beings have four major senses for reception of information: auditory, visual, tactile, and olfactory. Ordinarily, the most commonly used message channels are auditory and visual. The bulk of information available is on these two forms of sensory input for instructional purposes. Our discussion of the message channel sub-component will be limited to utilization of these two input channels. Before examining the research on oral and visual presentations, we will explore the rationale for variation of message channel. Following this, several strategies for decision-making will be presented along with procedures for gathering decision-making information.

Rationale

The purpose for varying message channel in responsive instruction is to identify and utilize the form of communication which best facilitates learning for the individual student. That is, the message channel employed should be responsive to student learning styles. This implies that some students may learn better if material is presented orally. This distinction between orally and visually presented material is most frequently related to verbal and spatial learning styles. The most frequent hypotheses have stipulated that verbally oriented learners will learn most effectively from oral and written presentations, while spatially oriented learners will profit more from visual presentations.

How are the characteristics of verbal and spatial instruction different? An obvious difference is that one relies on words more than the other. Spatially oriented instruction employs visuals, diagrams, and other forms of non-verbal presentations (e.g., equations). Frequently, spatial abilities are considered to be less conceptual and require less reasoning and, thus, are most frequently associated with low-ability students. Verbal abilities, on the other hand, are considered more abstract, more conceptual in nature, and to require more reasoning; verbal abilities are most frequently associated with high-ability students.

This distinction may be an artifact of the ordinary structure of our school curricula. For example, high-ability students are frequently tracked into curricula designed for the college-bound student. These curricula usually include a high number of verbally oriented courses, such as English, foreign language, science, and math. Ordinarily, these courses are taught via oral instruction with a heavy reliance on reading of textual material. Only students who have a long history of high achievement with similar content, who read well, and who have mastered verbal skills are admitted to such curricula.

On the other hand, students who have not done well via verbal presentations are placed in curricula which include quantitatively and qualitatively different content. Frequently, English content is less complex, science is more practical and less theoretical, and so forth. Greater use is made of visuals. Ordinarily, the visuals are quite simple and straightforward. Instruction is paced much more slowly and is focused on relatively elementary concepts.

As a result, neither group gets any extensive or realistic experience with alternate communication channels. The college-bound (more able?) students ordinarily are presented instruction which is heavily verbal and rarely visual. Similarly, less able students are presented instruction which is lower in verbal complexity and more visual in nature.

Because of the nature of this curriculum structure, two important questions are raised. The first is whether verbally oriented instruction is more likely to be successful with high-ability students. The second question relates to different content and revolves around the issue of whether verbally oriented instruction is more appropriate for some content (e.g., English) than others (e.g., math). The answer to both of these questions will have an impact on decisions to design instruction toward verbal or visual abilities. We will review some research results related to both these issues later, but first we will draw out the major issues.

Relative to the first question, it appears that more able students can profit from both verbal and spatial instruction. The issue is difficult, however, because verbal instruction can involve many variations. Cronbach and Snow (1977) made this point: "While educators have insufficient experience with spatial instruction to say just how this (maximization of spatially oriented instruction) is to be accomplished, we do have such experience with verbal instruction" (p. 282). They went on to point out that verbal instruction can be brief and complex or that concepts and ideas can be slowly and carefully constructed so that even students with lower verbal abilities can master the content. In all cases, the more elaborate verbal presentation may not be the best, since some students may find it tedious and overdone, and the more able students may profit more from organizing the concepts involved in a more active manner. Cronbach and Snow's point is that the same sort of differentiation may be done with visual materials. That is, materials can be "designed to either capitalize on the ability (forcing the student to exercise it) or to avoid demands on it" (p. 282). Research on variations in the structuring of spatially oriented instructional materials has not been done to any great extent. Thus, we do not know all the ramifications for instructional decisions related to using various types of spatial instruction.

The second issue revolves around the content of instruction. Essentially, the problem is whether verbal instruction may be detrimental to learning some content, whereas spatial instruction would be facilitative. There is the added complication of aptitudes interacting as well. In other words, some students may learn some content well via verbal instruction, but the same students may learn other content well via spatial instruction. It is not too difficult to generate examples of content where spatial instruction would logically be more productive. One such example is electronics. It is difficult to believe that a verbal presentation of a wiring diagram would be superior for any student to a spatial or schematic diagram. Certainly, the schematic diagram would be much more concise and perhaps even more easily read than a verbal description. The interaction of the electronic components would be more clearly represented in a schematic diagram than would seem possible in a verbal description. It may be that some components of what is ordinarily associated with verbal instruction may be more effectively presented spatially. For example, in grammar instruction, learning the relation between parts of speech in a sentence may be more easily understood with a diagram than with a verbal presentation.

To further complicate this issue, it may be that a student who acquires concepts such as beauty, addition, decision strategies, etc., well through verbal presentations may not learn other concepts or content as well verbally. It is not inconceivable for a highly verbal student to profit from visual presentations of relations between components in a process. Such spatial presentations are regularly used in content areas, such as computer science, which heavily emphasize the use of flow diagrams to represent processes and systems analysis to represent process component relations. Verbal presentations of information of this sort may be cumbersome even for highly verbal students.

It is a complex issue and one which is not easily resolved by the instructional decision-maker. The real crux of the problem, however, is not to identify and track spatial and verbal learners into spatially or verbally oriented content. The issue is to achieve "the *same* educational goal by alternative methods" (Cronbach and Snow, 1977, p. 280). That is, whatever the content or purpose, we need to identify the communication channel most responsive to student learning needs.

Research Results
The research on verbal versus spatial learning is not very helpful in terms of definitive answers to which is better for whom under what conditions. Once again, the instructional decision-maker is left largely to his or her own devices to sift through rather

inconclusive and sometimes contradictory research for aid in making instructional decisions. This lack of definitiveness stems largely from the type of research which has been conducted. That is, a great deal of research in this area, as in others, has sought consistent advantages of one form of communication over another, regardless of purpose or receptor characteristics. While few definitive results have emerged, more complex recent research has led several experts to formulate general guidelines relative to communication channel. These general guidelines are reviewed below in two categories: the relative effects of verbal versus spatial presentations and selection of mode of communication based on instructional purpose.

Verbal versus Spatial Presentations. Age, ability, and previous experience all appear to be important determinants in the relative effectiveness of verbal versus spatial or graphic presentations. A number of reviews of research have appeared in recent years which lead to conclusions about the interactions of these variables with the form of communication used in instruction (Cronbach and Snow, 1977; Levie and Dickie, 1973; and Travers, 1968). The following is a synthesis of research trends reported in these reviews.

Cronbach and Snow (1977) reviewed studies on the interactive effects of making instruction less verbal. They concluded that "the bulk of evidence again indicates interactions of vaguely defined general ability, and absence of expected effects of more specialized abilities" (p. 291). In other words, they found little evidence of students possessing either relatively verbal or relatively spatial learning styles. Most interactions were obtained on the basis of high versus low general ability.

One general conclusion drawn by Cronbach and Snow was that "easier, more symbolic treatments can reduce the advantage of those high in general ability . . . and therefore be advantageous for Lows" (p. 265). This was true for instruction in both mathematics and grammar but appeared to be more strongly associated with math instruction. That is, when symbolic presentations were made to students covering the math content, these were judged as easier and served low-ability students better than verbal presentations.

However, students who were of high ability tended to do well on both forms of instruction. Since the task of the instructional decision-maker is to make instruction responsive to student abilities or aptitudes, there is some reason to believe that communication channel variations will be nonproductive. However, additional research may lend more definition to the currently available body of literature, which will ease the task of identifying a match between specific abilities and effective communication channels.

Both Travers (1968) and Levie and Dickie (1973) devoted some attention to age. Travers concluded that "children in the lower elementary school grades, in contrast with upper grades, show a preference for simpler pictures and unrealistic coloring. In addition, as they grow older their preference for more realistic representations with more true-to-life colors increases" (p. 1). Levie and Dickie supported this conclusion. Thus, it appears that younger children (before grade three) (Travers and Alvarado, 1970) may require more verbally oriented instruction until they "learn how to 'read' pictures" (Levie and Dickie, 1973, p. 865). This conclusion most likely extends to the use of printed materials as well as pictures, since these young children are just beginning to acquire reading abilities.

Experience with visuals appears to be a third significant area of concern relative to the effectiveness of verbal versus visual materials. Learners who have had the opportunity to experience frequent use of visuals appear more able to learn effectively from them. As a result of continued experience with either verbally oriented or spatially oriented instruction, the learner is likely to develop a facility for and affinity to whichever approach is most frequently present. Shifts in communication channels in such situations may be disorienting and deleterious to learning, at least initially.

Communication Channel for Instructional Purposes. There appear to be a number of specific purposes for which verbal or spatial instruction are differentially most suitable. Let's review some of these:

1. Verbal presentations appear better than pictures for teaching abstract concepts.

2. Pictures are better for communicating a concept which has already been learned.

3. Simple pictures (i.e., line drawings) are as effective and sometimes more effective than elaborate or highly realistic pictures.

4. In cases where cue discrimination is being taught, however, realistic pictures are the most effective.

5. Verbal presentations appear to be superior to pictures for teaching generalizations.

6. Pictures appear to be superior to verbal presentations for teaching or facilitating creativity.

7. Pictures generally produce higher rates of recall than verbal presentations.

8. Printed materials allow for learner control of pace, sequence, and choice of learning time due to the referability of printed materials.

9. Learners must be guided to the' proper cues in pictures in order that their attention will be focused on relevant dimensions.

These general findings should provide some guidance to selection of communication channel based on instructional purpose. Most frequently, verbal abilities are estimated as either high or low on the basis of verbally oriented achievement tests, such as the Scholastic Aptitude Test or the California Test of Mental Maturity. Other instruments, such as the Differential Aptitude Test, have sub-sections which focus on both spatial and verbal aptitudes. When discrepancies are noted between general ability as indicated by composite scores on standardized achievement tests and actual performance as indicated by school achievement, this may be a clue to the use of an inappropriate message channel. Subsequent instruction utilizing alternate message channels may bring achievement in line with predictions based on standardized achievement tests.

Decision-Making

Two factors need to be considered in making decisions relative to communication channel; first, who is being taught and, second, what is being taught. The research indicates that older students may be more able than young students to handle spatial presentations. It also appears that generalizations and abstract concepts are more easily learned through verbal rather than spatial presentations. The specific properties of some content, however, may override some of these generalizations as well as the specific abilities of some learners. Pictures seem more appropriate for creative learning because the sequence of input is not structured. The complexity of verbal materials is also an important consideration. Students who handle abstractions well and who are adept at constructing organizations of information will probably do better with complex and difficult prose.

Native abilities (verbal versus spatial) may not be an important issue; at least not as important as a clear conceptualization on the part of the instructional designer of what he or she intends for students to learn. That is, high-ability students tend to do well with both visual and spatial instruction and vice versa for low-ability students. This may mean that students need to be taught how to maximize their own learning from both forms of communication. Students should be taught how to learn from verbal as well as spatial presentations. Students low in verbal (and general) ability may need to be taught how to extract main ideas from textual material as well as how to organize thoughts and ideas. Students may also need to be taught how to discriminate relevant from irrelevant information in graphic and pictorial presentations. In other words, students, regardless of ability, need to be taught how to most effectively receive information regardless of the communication channel employed.

Essentially, the same decision considerations should be employed with other senses as with verbal or visual presentations. That is, the form of communication should meet content and student needs. The senses of touch and smell/taste may be as effective, or in some cases more effective, as sight and hearing. For example, it may be easier to teach discrimination of substances of similar appearance by taste or touch than through either verbal or visual means. Touch and taste may also be very effective means of teaching creativity by asking students to describe the "taste" of a sound or the "feel" of an emotion. True understanding of any concept, abstract or concrete, may be most readily accomplished by encouraging students to employ all their senses to define or describe what they are asked to learn.

Finally, as with most instructional decisions, there is no absolute certainty that any communication channel will be responsive to all students at all times. It is, therefore, a good idea to offer alternative channels for all instruction. That is, the same concept, idea, information, or value should be taught via several communication channels when possible.

Decision-Making Information

1. *Standardized Tests.* Success on most achievement tests relies very heavily on verbal abilities. High scores should correlate with relatively high achievement.

2. *Achievement History.* If students have a record of success with either verbal or spatially oriented instruction, this should indicate a responsiveness to the communication channel which has led to success.

3. *Student Questionnaire.* While not too reliable, students may be asked to describe the type of learning experiences they like best and from which they profit the most. Such reports should be validated with other sources of information but may provide some clues to identification of responsive communication channels.

Summary

Message channel decisions determine the sensory mode through which the instructional message will be communicated to the students. We concentrated heavily on verbal and spatial modes of communication; it appears that differential use of communication mode may impact on student learning. However, decisions in this sub-component are quite complex, and the nature of interaction between communication mode and student characteristics is not well-known. The best advice appears to be to select a communication mode which conforms to the purposes of instruction. In general, age, ability, and previous experience of students should be considered as well as the characteristics of the content.

Decisions, then, should be based on what is being taught and who is being taught. A variety of sources of information may be useful in determining the communication mode which will be most responsive to student needs.

References

Cronbach, L.J., and Snow, R.E. *Aptitudes and Instructional Methods.* New York: Irvington Publishers, Inc., 1977.

Levie, W.H., and Dickie, K.E. The Analysis and Application of Media. In R.M.W. Travers (Ed.), *Second Handbook of Research on Teaching.* Chicago: Rand McNally College Publishing Company, 1973.

Travers, R.M.W. Theory of Perception and the Design of Audiovisual Materials. Paper presented at the Faculty Seminar on Educational Media, Bucknell University, April, 1968.

Travers, R.M.W., and Alvarado, V. The Design of Pictures for Teaching Children in Elementary School. *A V Communications Review*, 1970, *27*, 101-109.

10

Instructional Strategies

Instructional strategies is the next sub-component and includes decisions on how the student and content are to be brought together. Any technique for facilitating positive interaction between student and content may be an appropriate strategy. The propriety of any strategy basically rests on how well learning is facilitated. Thus, once again, we will have to consider student characteristics, content, logic, and empirical data in decision-making. A major problem with decision-making about instructional strategies is that there is an almost infinite variety of possible strategies, and within various strategies, a large number of variations. That is, a lecture may be organized around a number of different approaches, so that the characteristics of one lecture vary widely from another. Another difficulty is in determining the relative merits of any single strategy. In this chapter, we will review some basic distinctions which can be applied to strategies; review relevant research which may be useful for decision-making; and develop a strategy for making instructional strategy decisions. Upon completion of this chapter, you should know how to make instructional strategy decisions.

Rationale
Our basic purpose is to select instructional strategies which will be most responsive to student needs. At this point in our decision-making process, we have developed a well-specified structure of learning and have also considered time dimensions and message channel. The selection of a strategy is a major step toward

incorporating these variables into specific teacher actions which will result in the necessary learning conditions being present to maximize the probability of student learning. In effect, we are specifying the behavioral parameters of the learning conditions.

The sub-component, instructional strategies, is defined as the *specific actions taken by the teacher to bring about the productive interaction of students and content.* The first phrase we will look at is *specific actions taken by the teacher.* You will recall that we are using the term teacher in a generic sense, so that it includes any planned activity which brings student and content together. In the general sense that "teacher" is used in the instructional exchange, it includes all delivery decisions. Here, however, we are referring to specific actions which initiate and continue student-content interaction. In other words, we are focusing on the observable behaviors of the teacher which result in this contact between student and content.

Obviously, many such actions are possible, but these fall into two major categories. The first are those actions which require some form of direct human intervention to effect student-content interaction. A lecture would be an example of a strategy in this category. The second category consists of actions which do not necessarily involve direct human intervention. In this category, students are brought into contact with content via printed materials, programmed texts, audiotapes, etc. In both categories, the strategies must be carefully thought out, chosen, planned, and delivered. The selection of strategies in one category over another must be based on student need, available resources, and probability of success.

The next phrase is *to bring about the productive interaction of students and content.* Enough has already been said about the role of strategies in bringing students and content together. It should be stressed, however, that this interaction must be productive. Productive means that students should be learning what was intended from this interaction. This requires a sensitivity on the part of the teacher to the effects of strategies on students as a group and as individuals. The teacher is well advised to be diligent to both productive and deleterious effects of any strategy selected.

Careful selection should preclude the choice of a very harmful strategy, and this is the reason for considering strategy decisions in light of as much information as possible and practical.

A major problem with the selection of a specific strategy or teacher action is that there is such a wide variety of strategies. To develop an exhaustive list of these strategies would require an inordinate amount of space. And such a list would not be very helpful, since the specific actions may bear no direct relation to specific expected learning outcomes. It would certainly be nice if strategy decisions could be made on the basis of well-formulated prescriptions. However, such prescriptions rarely hold up across all instructional situations and inevitably lead to a false sense of "doing what is right." In reality, what is right in terms of a strategy decision is based on what works for the students involved in the particular situation to promote learning of the content being taught. In other words, the decision on strategies is quite idiosyncratic and must be appropriate for the learners and content involved. Generally, such decisions will not conform to "all-purpose" prescriptions.

To illustrate this point, let's look at an often cited article by Rosenshine and Furst (1971) which appeared in the proceedings of a symposium sponsored by the American Educational Research Association. In their review, Rosenshine and Furst reviewed process-product studies which investigated the relationship between teacher behaviors (process) and student learning (product). They identified 11 process variables which appeared related to student achievement: clarity, variability, enthusiasm, task oriented and/or businesslike behavior, student opportunity to learn criterion material, use of student ideas and general indirectness, criticism, use of structuring comments, types of questions, probing, and level of difficulty of instruction. It has been implied from this review that the presence of these teacher variables would result in greater probability of student learning. However, this implication has not been supported. In fact, the prescriptive nature of this approach has led to many erroneous conclusions of the sort that "teacher clarity results in higher student achievement."

It may be that clarity does lead to achievement in some cases; however, what is lacking here is a rationale for being clear and a theoretical framework to specify what is clear and what is not. There are situations where lack of clarity may promote greater learning. For example, high-ability students with strong verbal aptitudes may profit more from less clear materials in that the able student who "organizes for himself will probably learn more than when he passively absorbs premasticated materials" (Cronbach and Snow, 1977, p. 282). In summary, "process-product variables must be interwoven into the fabric of the complex learning process to be meaningful" (Giles and Sherman, 1978, p. 20).

Our perception is that the teacher needs a conceptual basis for making decisions about strategies. We have maintained this need for a conceptual basis for decision-making relative to all decisions. However, stressing the point here seems particularly important, since teaching and instruction have a history of being viewed as the specific in-class behaviors of teachers. From our perspective in responsive instruction, these actions are but one piece of an extensive decision-making process.

In order to assist in the development of this conceptual basis for making decisions about strategies, we will do three things. First, we will examine the functions of strategies; second, we will look at a framework for making strategy decisions; third, we will review some rather general alternative strategy approaches.

To review briefly, our purpose within the strategies sub-component is to determine how to get students to learn the necessary content to be able to perform the stated terminal performances. The "how" which is decided upon should conform with previous decisions on structuring learning; time; and message channel. In addition, we must be concerned with student characteristics, empirical data, and logic in making strategy decisions. Any strategy is likely to be successful or unsuccessful. The selection of a strategy should be made from a series of reasonable alternatives which are consistent with needed learning conditions, teacher abilities, and teacher beliefs about how learning takes place.

Functions of Strategies

Strategies serve two major functions in the delivery of instruction. The first is the control and regulation of student-content interaction. The second is the management of the instructional environment. Let's examine each of these functions in terms of the importance of each in an instructional situation.

Control and Regulation. The first function which a strategy can provide for is the control and regulation of student-content interaction. Recall that one reason for designing instruction is to speed up the learning process. That is, uncontrolled trial-and-error learning is time-consuming, usually quite inefficient, and does not always lead to a desired outcome. A major purpose for planning instruction is to establish control over the learning in order to increase the probability of positive outcomes. This control is essential if instruction is to be both effective and efficient.

The control which is a function of the strategy is in terms of the structure of the content, learning conditions, time elements, and message channel. In other words, the teacher wishes to control the instructional program so that the students receive information and process it in an orderly way. Without this kind of control, previous decisions relative to structure and delivery would be without impact. Strategies provide a mechanism for implementing previous decisions about content and learner interaction with this content.

Regulation is also a necessary element in instruction. Here we refer to procedures to maintain the flow of learning through instruction. Landa (1974) referred to regulation as the process of using feedback to maintain "some state of the controlled system within some given limits" (p. 32). Functionally, this regulation is made possible through the use of strategies which can be adjusted to some extent in order to be responsive to changes in the learner.

Let's look at an example of control and regulation. Suppose we select a strategy, such as example giving, in order to facilitate student interaction with content, such as concept learning. We can establish much control over the interaction by presenting concept instances first and non-instances second and systematically varying critical dimensions of the concept in the instances and non-instances (e.g., see Becker, Engelmann, and Thomas, 1971, pp. 374-375). This is obviously a highly controlled presentation of content, such that learners are presented with only one relevant dimension at a time. Furthermore, this control, embedded in the strategy of example giving, clearly places the teacher in charge of how students interact with the content. Such a strategy would be decided upon because the content involved concept learning, specific types of examples (verbal, spatial, or both), appeared appropriate, and so forth.

Regulation can be added to this example if we consider student reactions to the examples given. Thus, the focus of regulation is the student; regulatory activities are modifications of structure and delivery decisions. For example, if the students grasped the concept quickly, the additional examples could be deleted. Student attention could be maintained by a variety of examples if appropriate or by variations in time devoted to deliver objectives. Regulation connotes subtle changes in these decision areas which modify planned activities in light of student feedback.

A good strategy will provide the teacher with the means to implement previous decisions so that control can be exerted over the instructional program. This control allows students to be guided through the learning program under optimal learning conditions. Regulation will allow the instructional process to be modified in minor ways in order to be responsive to student needs. A critical factor in making strategy decisions is the selection of strategies which provide for optimal opportunities for regulation and control.

Management of the Instructional Environment. The second function of a strategy is to provide for the management of the instructional environment. In almost all cases, the situations in which instruction is delivered are quite complex. This complexity comes from several sources, each of which increases the complexity. Groups of students are made up of individuals who are different on a number of dimensions in terms of learning characteristics and social and personality factors. Since the classroom is a social situation, some organization is required to keep things running smoothly. The same requirement holds for situations in which individuals work by themselves, because it is necessary to initiate and maintain student-content interaction in an organized manner.

What is required is an organizational strategy in which learning can be managed in a realistic manner. Five key elements have been identified as necessary for effective classroom organization and management (Sherman, 1978). These are: maintenance of social order; presentation of content; motivation of students; record-keeping; and planning. The strategy selected must include these elements in order for the learning program to be effectively implemented.

The basic idea is that the learning situation must run smoothly in order to provide an atmosphere conducive to learning. Essentially, we are adding a second level of instructional organization to the planning and decision-making considered to this point. For example, it is one thing to activate student attention in a particular instructional situation. It is quite another matter to maintain an atmosphere conducive to activating attention. If students are swinging from the light fixtures, it will be difficult to activate their attention, regardless of the strategy chosen. The goal of environmental management is to create a milieu in which learning can occur.

Let's briefly review the five elements identified by Sherman. The importance of the maintenance of social order seems obvious enough. Not much can be accomplished in an atmosphere of disorder and confusion, regardless of the quality of instructional decisions. Presentation of content has been dealt with previously, and its importance should also be well-established. Motivation of students is necessary in order to maintain attention, interest, and willingness to learn, regardless of the content involved. The goal here is to create a learning set or expectation among students as a motivating factor. Record-keeping is viewed as a necessity in order to provide sufficient information availability to make decisions regarding student achievement and instructional quality. These data are necessary, in other words, for evaluation and revision purposes. More will be said about these functions in the chapters on evaluation and remediation. The final element is planning, which includes the process of planning new instruction as well as revising and moderating current instructional decisions.

The two areas not included in detail in other portions of the responsive instruction model are motivation and social order. Before addressing these, however, we will return to the point made earlier about the two levels of strategy considerations. At one level, we have considered strategies as the actions which bring students and content into interaction. We call this a micro-level, since the purposes are of a very specific nature. That is, specific content is delivered to students in a specific manner for a specific and well-defined purpose as stated in the objectives.

The second level we call the macro-level, since the purposes are more global in nature in that they cut across all learning. These purposes are those expressed in the management elements. They are necessary regardless of the specific learning situation.

The advantages of macro-level strategies are that they provide, first, a series of alternatives which may be useful for a variety of specific strategies. Second, they provide a structural framework in which micro-strategies may be implanted. We will not review these macro-strategies, since many are described elsewhere, such as in *The Instructional Design Library,* edited by Langdon (1978, 1980). It should be noted that these strategies vary widely in terms of purpose and operation. They mandate varying roles by teachers in that some stress planning, others motivation, others social order, etc. Therefore, the organizing and managing strategy which is selected should be based on teacher abilities, student needs, delivery demands, and the structure of the learning involved. In other words, the macro-strategy must be consistent with the intentions and overall or holistic conceptualization of the instructional program.

A final note about management of the instructional environment: In many ways, the selection of a management strategy will determine the practicality of the instruction designed. It is of little consequence to have a well-designed program of instruction if it cannot be implemented. It is critical, therefore, to consider the environment into which the instructional program will be placed. Clearly, this is an area over which the teacher has control and, therefore, can make effective decisions which will facilitate learning.

Let's look at some procedures which may be incorporated into management approaches which may facilitate social order and student motivation. Perhaps the most extensive literature on social order is in the area of behavior modification, which is essentially a technology for implementation of principles derived from behavioral psychology research. There are excellent sources which explain this technology in great detail (e.g., Sulzer and Mayer, 1972; Vargas, 1977). The major principle upon which this technology is based is positive reinforcement. That is, behaviors which are followed by reinforcing events tend to increase. A wealth of research supports the efficacy of using positive reinforcement. The critical issues are to identify effective reinforcers and to use these reinforcers in the correct manner. Motivating students is also addressed by behaviorally oriented psychologists. Again, reinforcement is the major tool for motivating students.

Other psychologists, such as Smith (1975) and Bruner (1966), have stressed the importance of relevance as a factor in motivation. Smith (1975) stated, "In fact, it can be asserted that all children who have not been spoilt for learning can be interested in anything, provided two conditions are met. The first condition is that the learning situation makes sense, and the second is that it contains novelty" (p. 232). Motivation should be viewed as a complex notion consisting of many elements as well as highly variable between individuals. Perhaps the best advice, and it is advice with little direction, is to take whatever actions are possible to make the learning situation exciting and rewarding so that it is a place where students want to be. Depending on your personal orientation, this may be done by systematically reinforcing students, by challenging them, by sheer force of personality, or by creating inharmonious situations which students must resolve. The point is that whatever decisions are made, the actions emanating from these decisions should be a regular and systematic feature incorporated into the management strategy.

Decision Framework

The actual selection of a strategy requires the consideration of a great deal of information. So much information must be considered that a decision framework or strategy is necessary in order to, first, consider the requisite information; second, generate sufficient appropriate alternatives; and, third, select a suitable alternative. Our basic framework for decision-making about strategies will be to first acquire needed decision information from all pertinent sources. This will require the identification of those sources of information. The next step is to coordinate data with strategy categories. This should facilitate the generation of relevant characteristics of strategies which will correspond to the demands of the instructional situation. Third, a number of alternatives should be generated in order to provide a range of strategies. Finally, a strategy or several strategies must be selected as the most likely to meet the instructional and learner needs. A two-dimensional framework for decision-making about strategies is presented in Figure 10.1. We will examine these two dimensions, beginning with decision information, and then look at the dimension of instructional strategy categories.

Decision information includes all categories of data or decisions made relative to the variables included in the left-hand column under decision information in Figure 10.1. These represent decisions already made and other factors which contribute to the selection of strategies as these relate to the dimensions across the top of Figure 10.1, strategy categories. The objective here is to systematically consider decisions and resources which will affect the characteristics of the strategy selected.

Decision information includes five categories of information. The first is structure; of course, we are referring to decisions made in the structuring learning component. Of particular interest here are decisions made relative to learning conditions, since the strategy selected will determine to a great extent how these conditions are made available. The content components and instructional elements should also be included as contributors to the decision process. A reanalysis of the structure is not being suggested, since the structure of learning is well-established. What is necessary is to keep this structure in mind as strategy decisions are made.

The next category is the student. Student characteristics and

Figure 10.1

Decision Framework for Generating
Strategy Characteristics

	Strategy Categories			
	Teacher Action	Media	Students/ Others	Outside Resources
Structure				
Student				
Empirical Data				
Time/Message Channel				
Teacher Abilities				

(Decision Information)

aptitudes should be included to guide the decision process. Student success with strategies used in previous instruction should be one major consideration. Another should be any special characteristics identified among students, such as a need for large amounts of feedback or desire for independent learning. The third category is empirical data which can contribute information about specific strategies. Here we are focusing on any characteristics of a strategy which have been supported by empirical evidence as facilitative of learning. These data may be of many different kinds and of various degrees of usefulness.

Time and message channel decisions have been made prior to strategy decisions and, thus, must be considered when making a decision on a strategy. That is, the strategy must be consistent with decisions made about time and message channel. For example, if a decision has been made to pace instruction slowly and to utilize both visual and verbal communication channels, the strategy must be able to accommodate these decisions.

The final category is teacher abilities. We need to consider abilities in two ways. First, a teacher is not ordinarily a multi-talented individual who can do everything well. Inevitably, teachers develop a teaching style through which they capitalize on the particular abilities they have developed. Some teachers, for example, can deliver excellent lectures, while others do not have the personality or histrionic abilities which contribute to effective lectures. It would be foolish for a teacher to continually lecture if he or she does this poorly. Therefore, the abilities necessary to effectively implement a strategy should be identified and matched with the teacher's abilities. No strategy which does not match well should be selected. Second, the resources necessary to deliver a strategy should be studied. If the resources are not available, or substitutions cannot be made with available resources, then the strategy should be eliminated from consideration.

The second dimension in the decision framework is called strategy categories and includes four categories. Strategy categories are the observable characteristics of the strategy or the specific characteristics which identify the strategy. For example, discussion may be identified as a strategy by the leadership of the teacher, frequency of student contributions, and so forth. However, the strategy—discussion—would be selected because the decision information indicated that a strategy which included a high degree of student participation and teacher leadership would be appropriate. In other words, the selection of a strategy is based on the characteristics generated. These strategy categories are used to generate strategy characteristics within the cells of Figure 10.1, which may then be used to generate strategy alternatives conforming to these characteristics.

The first category is teacher action. Our purpose is to determine the nature (direct or indirect) of teacher action and the characteristics of this involvement. What we are doing here is crossing the decision information categories with strategy categories in order to generate strategy characteristics. In the cell which includes teacher action and structure, we would consider the characteristics of teacher action, which would lead to student learning given the particular structure of learning. For example, suppose a higher-order rule were being taught which required learning conditions of recall, problem presentation, and demonstration opportunities. What characteristics would fit in this cell? We could have direct or indirect teacher action, stimulate recall by questions, review, demonstration, etc. All of these strategy characteristics should be considered as part of this cell. As other characteristics are entered in other cells, the number of characteristics which appear in every cell will be reduced. It is those characteristics common to all the cells in Figure 10.1 which will be the major descriptors used to generate alternative strategies.

We will not exemplify the process of generating strategy characteristics for each cell. It should be clear that the purpose here is to identify the required characteristics of a strategy rather than the strategy itself. We do this because a strategy is a means to an end and as such should be selected because the strategy will lead to the end. The goal or end in using a strategy is to facilitate learning of specific content oriented toward certain objectives. As a result, we must choose a strategy through which the necessary learning conditions can be provided. This can be done only by first considering what conditions and characteristics must be present and then choosing a strategy which conforms to these requirements. We are suggesting that these characteristics can be generated by considering the interaction of decision information with strategy categories.

The remaining strategy categories are described below. Media includes the use of audio, audio-visual, and visual techniques and procedures which can be incorporated into a strategy. Particular attention may be given to the type of media employed and the advantages of the use of media. The next category is students and others. This category may or may not be frequently used; however, it is clear that students and others (parents, older students, etc.) may contribute to learning and also be useful to consider in identifying strategy characteristics. Finally, outside resources refer to any resource outside the learning situation which may be included as a part of the strategy and hence be useful in generating characteristics.

Following the generation of these characteristics, alternative strategies must be identified which fit the characteristics. Ordinarily this requires some creativity and is enhanced by a broad knowledge of possible strategies. This includes knowledge of specific instructional strategies, empirical data about the strategies, and specific characteristics of the strategies. Many times, alternative strategies cannot be selected from a predetermined menu but must be developed in order to accommodate the characteristics identified. For example, the characteristics could indicate that the strategy should be verbal and spatial, teacher-directed, paced quickly with many examples, and include frequent opportunities for student feedback. It would be difficult to find a strategy which included all these characteristics. However, it is possible to generate alternatives which would meet these demands. A lecture using overhead visuals and lots of questions could be one. A film with frequent attention-directing statements and discussion could be another. A programmed book with many illustrations could be yet another. It is probably more accurate to say these strategies are created by the teacher, since they are ordinarily designed to meet the specific needs of the students and content involved in a particular situation. As a result, most strategies are relatively idiosyncratic combinations of teacher actions which conform to the strategy characteristics generated.

Selection of an alternative must be based on the probable success of the strategy. However, the final selection decision is basically a matter of teacher choice and professional judgment. In most cases, it is a good idea to include more than one strategy in order to provide maximum opportunity to every student.

Instructional Strategy Alternatives

It has been stated a number of times in this chapter that strategy decisions cannot be made from prescriptions. In addition, we have seen how the selection of a strategy must be based on the characteristics of what must be done with students to make the interaction of student and content productive. The decision on a specific strategy results in the synthesis of these characteristics into a strategy which fits the students and content. Smith (1975) made the same point in this way: "I feel quite strongly that teachers should not be given general prescriptions about what they ought to do; rather they should be given the information that they need—about children and the nature of the learning tasks—so that they can make their own decisions about what to do on a particular occasion with respect to a particular child. I am not saying that teachers should not learn all they can about alternative instructional procedures and materials, the tools of their trade, but this knowledge is useless, even dangerous, unless the teacher can make a sound decision about what the methodology is trying to achieve, the demands it will make on a child, and the particular requirements, capacities, and limitations of a child at a particular time" (p. 6). What we are missing at this point is some idea of the range of strategy alternatives available. In this section, we will review some strategy alternatives in terms of rather broad distinctions. These will serve as general approaches to strategies into which almost any specific action may be placed.

Direct vs. Indirect Instruction. Flanders (1965) distinguished between direct and indirect instruction based on the nature of influence exerted by verbal statements teachers made in the classroom. Direct influence, according to Flanders, "consists of those verbal statements of the teacher that restrict freedom of action, by focusing attention on a problem, interjecting teacher authority, or both" (p. 9). Flanders included lecturing, direction-giving, criticizing, and "justifying his own use of authority" as examples of direct influences. "Indirect influence consists of those verbal statements of the teacher that expand a student's freedom of action by encouraging his verbal participation and initiative" (p. 9). Question-asking, clarifying ideas, and feelings, praise, and encouragement were identified by Flanders as indirect influences. Flanders proposed that indirect verbal influences were more appropriate, since these tend to free students and help them find solutions to their own problems. Flanders' approach was basically deductive and based on a tradition of investigation of social interaction in the classroom. There is relatively little support for indirect teaching as a meritorious approach to increasing student achievement (e.g., Barr and Dreeben, 1977). However, the idea continues to have a strong conceptual appeal, and it is equally accurate to say that there is little research which shows this approach to be damaging.

Direct instruction was described by Rosenshine (1976) in terms of teacher structure, a more comprehensive approach than Flanders' attention to verbal interaction. Direct instruction consists of supervised lesson and workbook activities; little free time; teacher dominance over the selection and timing of activities; narrow and factual questions; and immediate teacher reinforcement of correct responses. The learning atmosphere is described as very businesslike and centered on teacher-organized questions and materials.

Rosenshine (1976, 1978) has reviewed a number of variables as these relate to achievement in mathematics and reading, centering on academic engaged time and content covered. Rosenshine (1978) limited the use of direct instruction to "didactic ends, that is, for instruction toward rational, specific analytic goals which appear on the reading tests we are currently using" (p. 9a). The research Rosenshine (1978) reviewed was strongly in favor of direct instruction. He concluded that "the more successful teacher is one who structures and selects activities, who obtains a large number of academic engaged minutes each day, who tends to ask questions which have specific answers in a controlled practice format, who places students in groups where they are supervised by the teacher, and who does this in a controlled but convivial classroom" (p. 21).

Inductive vs. Deductive. The basic issue which separates these two approaches is whether students should process information in a highly self-generated manner (inductive) or from an organized presentation (deductive). Bruner (1966) is probably the most visible proponent of discovery learning, in which instruction is arranged so that students can discover an organization of the content. This is based on the idea that all new knowledge is related to previous knowledge in terms of categories and structure. This kind of organization cannot be imposed or dictated. Bruner recommends a spiral curriculum, which is not a sequenced series of steps but rather a presentation of the same material at different levels at different times. Students are encouraged to organize information by inducing curiosity and by forming and testing hypotheses. In other words, students are encouraged to actively process information.

Ausubel (1968) believes that new information is more effectively acquired and stored when the information has meaning for the learner. Meaningfulness is enhanced when the content is organized in a way that facilitates acquisition. This is accomplished by explicitly organizing the information into a logical order of superordinate and subordinate components. The organization provides a meaningful structure in which the information can be stored by the learner and more easily retrieved on demand. When these meaningful structures already exist, instruction should be oriented to this organizational structure in an explicit way. When these organizers do not exist, then instruction should begin with expository organizers which define the inherent structure of the information. The approach is a deductive one, since the major characteristic of the organizers is from the most general element of the information to the most specific.

It should be noted that research on these two approaches is equivocal at best. The approach one takes in delivery of instruction should be based on the purposes of the instruction and the students involved. The real issue is not which is best, but rather what is best for whom and under what conditions.

Learning Theory. The final strategy alternative we will consider is not a strategy alternative at all. However, learning theories do provide a basis for making strategy decisions. The value and role of beliefs about how learning occurs have been emphasized previously. The general and specific features of a learning theory can influence every instructional decision, since the design of instruction should be consistent with whatever beliefs are held about how learning occurs. This is clearly true for the selection of strategies.

That is, the strategy selected must be consistent with such parameters of the learning process as whether learning requires relatively active or passive learner involvement, the nature of the learner involvement, the manner in which involvement is facilitated, and the role of the teacher in effecting learner-content interaction. Ordinarily, theories will not prescribe specific strategies. However, theories do ordinarily include descriptions of the learning process and conditions which promote learning. These formulations may be used by decision-makers to generate strategies which conform to the theoretical position. So, once again, stress the importance of developing and using a learning theory, either someone else's or your own must be stressed to form a foundation for instructional decision-making. A learning theory may be helpful in at least two specific ways in making strategy decisions. First, the theory can direct you to relevant empirical research regarding strategies and, as a result, your efforts can be focused on specific issues of importance for the strategy decisions you will make. Second, the theory can be generative in the sense that a specific strategy may be suggested by a theory that will incorporate the data generated by the decision framework.

Summary

Strategy decisions determine the teacher behaviors which will result in student-content interaction. The purposes of a strategy are to provide control over this interaction and to effect an environment conducive to learning. Strategies cannot be based on prescriptions, since each instructional situation is unique. Instead, strategies must be generated to be consistent with the content, learners, resources, and the teacher involved. A four-step procedure was suggested for the generation of strategies. The first step involves gathering together five categories of decision information. The next step is the consideration of these data in terms of four strategy categories in order to generate strategy characteristics. Third, specific teacher actions must be generated which correspond to these characteristics. Fourth, a strategy or several strategies must be decided upon from the alternative generated. The process is analytic and final selection of a strategy rests on teacher judgment about what will work best for the students involved.

References

Ausubel, D.P. *Educational Psychology: A Cognitive View.* New York: Holt, Rinehart, and Winston, 1968.

Barr, R., and Dreeben, R. Instruction in Classrooms. In L.S. Shulman (Ed.), *Review of Research in Education, Vol. 5.* Itasca, Ill.: F.E. Peacock Publishers, Inc., 1977.

Becker, W.C., Engelmann, S., and Thomas, D.R. *Teaching: A Course in Applied Psychology.* Chicago: SRA, 1971.

Bruner, J.S. *Toward a Theory of Instruction.* New York: W.W. Norton and Co., 1966.

Cronbach, L.J., and Snow, R.E. *Aptitudes and Instructional Methods.* New York: Irvington Publishers, Inc., 1977.

Flanders, N.A. *Teacher Influence, Pupil Attitudes, and Achievement.* Washington, D.C.: U.S. Dept. of Health, Education, and Welfare, 1965.

Giles, M.B., and Sherman, T.M. An Analytic Review of Teacher Clarity. Unpublished manuscript. College of Education, Virginia Polytechnic Institute and State University, 1978.

Landa, L.N. *Instructional Regulation and Control.* Englewood Cliffs, N.J.: Educational Technology Publications, 1974.

Langdon, D.G. *The Instructional Design Library* (20 volumes).

Englewood Cliffs, N.J.: Educational Technology Publications, 1978. Second set of 20 volumes, 1980.

Rosenshine, B.V. Classroom Instruction. In N.L. Gage (Ed.), *The Psychology of Teaching Methods, the Seventy-Fifth Yearbook of the National Society for the Study of Education.* Chicago: The University of Chicago Press, 1976.

Rosenshine, B.V. Academic Engaged Time, Content Covered, and Direct Instruction. Paper presented at the annual conference of the American Association of Colleges for Teacher Education, Chicago, 1978.

Rosenshine, B.V., and Furst, N. Research in Teacher Performance Criteria. In B.O. Smith (Ed.), *Research in Teacher Education.* Englewood Cliffs, N.J.: Prentice-Hall, Inc., 1971.

Sherman, T.M. Classroom Strategies for Organizing and Managing Individualized Instruction. Unpublished manuscript, College of Education, Virginia Polytechnic Institute and State University, 1978.

Smith, F. *Comprehension and Learning.* New York: Holt, Rinehart, and Winston, 1975.

Sulzer, B., and Mayer, R.G. *Behavior Modification Procedures for School Personnel.* Hinsdale, Ill.: The Dryden Press, 1972.

Vargas, J.S. *Behavioral Psychology for Teachers.* New York: Harper and Row, 1977.

11

Space

The sub-component of space includes all physical space, properties of space, and arrangement of space used for delivery of instruction. In essence, this sub-component consists of the physical aspects of the instructional environment. In other words, our interest here is on what the effects on learning might be if instructional space were differentially arranged. The effects of various spatial arrangements and the physical environment have not been studied widely in education. However, there has been a good deal of interest in this area in social and ecological psychology. In this chapter, we will review some pertinent portions of this research; examine the research for educational implications; and look at some decision-making guidelines for determining how to arrange instructional space.

Let us begin by affirming that data exist which appear to support the notion that variations in physical space may affect learning and classroom interaction. (See Knirk, 1979.) In addition, it appears that these physical environmental effects are characteristically similar to other variables in the way that humans are affected by them. That is, they are individual in nature and likely to vary in effect between individuals based on aptitude variables and within individuals based on psychological changes.

Color, for example, appears to be an important feature of the spatial environment. Drew (1971) reported several studies which indicated that lighter colors foster more and faster movement. Thus, it would seem that light colors should be used in active spaces, while darker colors should be used in quiet spaces.

Room arrangement is a critical feature of space. The thrust of research on room arrangement is that space should be arranged to suit specific purposes. For example, if the goal of the seating arrangement is to increase student-to-student discussion, certain arrangements may be better depending on the number of students involved. Opposing seating appears to generate most discussion when two people are involved. However, when distance between the two parties increases to more than five feet and exceeds the side-by-side distance, then ordinary rows of chairs are probably better.

Other variations in furniture arrangement can also promote increases in specific behaviors. For example, an "open" versus "closed" arrangement can facilitate social conversation and approaches. Several studies involving furniture arrangement have been done in mental health facilities in which some arrangements have facilitated greater interaction among patients. These arrangements generally involved the elimination of barriers between people.

Weinstein (1976) studied the physical design of a second-third grade "informal" classroom in order to determine if changes in the physical structure would affect student behavior. She studied student behavior patterns for two weeks and then analyzed her data relative to the teacher's stated goals. The classroom was rectangular in shape, 22 feet by 32 feet. The room was divided into seven "areas." Five of these were subject matter areas, and the other two were labeled "file" and "corner." Children were free to choose areas, where they worked on independent activities. The teacher spent the majority of her time "meeting with individuals and small groups to introduce lessons and activities and to check on academic progress" (p. 4). An analysis of the data "demonstrated vividly that all areas of the room were not being used to full advantage" (p. 14).

There were several instructional goals and criteria which were essential to the success of the classroom program. First, all areas had to attract their share of students. Otherwise, some areas would be overcrowded and others under-used. This was not the case, according to Weinstein's data. The corner, science, and games areas were under-used and restricted in the types of activities which occurred in each (i.e., no reading or writing in the science area). Also, girls avoided the science area. Second, the materials and equipment in the room had to be attractive enough to involve the children. The data, however, "indicated that the children were not using the manipulative materials and equipment to any great extent, despite the fact that this was one of the teacher's major goals" (Weinstein, 1976, p. 14). An additional problem was that children were not utilizing the reading area well. This area had the highest frequency of large motor behavior as well as a great deal of "looking" and "communication." This occurred in spite of the teacher's wishes that it be a quiet space for reading.

Several changes in room arrangement were implemented, which resulted in a change in the use of space in the room. Shelves were added so that materials could be more attractively displayed and more easily accessible in the science and games areas. The reading area was modified by adding some smaller spaces to the large reading area. Writing surfaces were added in the games area in the form of a table and stools. The relative size of the file area was decreased.

All changes were instituted during a long weekend so that when the children returned the classroom modifications were in place. Post-change results indicated that the distribution of students across the room "shifted considerably." The reading and corner areas remained about the same, but utilization in the art, math, and science areas increased. The file area was used about one-half as much as during the pre-change period. The kinds of student behaviors also changed somewhat with "fidget," "large physical activity," and "passive behavior" unobserved during the post-change period.

Drew (1971) reported data which led him to conclude that "spatial and design configurations that are simple and symmetrical are preferable. If, however, one were working with highly creative students, a more complex-asymmetrical environment might be more productive" (p. 459).

Perhaps the major conclusion to be drawn from existing research studies is that space should be designed to conform to teacher goals. It is relatively clear from the Weinstein study that alterations in spatial arrangement can facilitate classroom instructional goals. The room modifications made by Weinstein were relatively minor and inexpensive. Yet, they resulted in classroom behavior patterns more closely approximating ideal space utilization by students. Other implications can be drawn which are also in line with the reported data. For example, if a classroom goal is to facilitate student interaction, furniture should be arranged so as to provide for "intimate" areas where students can face one another. On the other hand, discussion can be suppressed by separating students. Quiet, independent study can be facilitated with small areas of rather dark colors. Student-teacher interaction can be made more possible with an open arrangement with few barriers between teacher and student.

Decisions on Spatial Arrangement

The main goal in spatial arrangement is to make the space conform to instructional goals as well as to meet individual student needs. There is little research at present on the interactions which may occur between space arrangements and student characteristics. However, a few interactions may be hypothesized. One of these is between symmetry/complexity and student creativity. Creative students seem to prefer more complex, less symmetrical arrangements. Another is between color, size, and student activity. Very active students may profit more than less active students from small spaces of darker colors. However, since these relationships are hypothetical, it may be best at this point to base space configurations mostly on program goals.

This, of course, requires a careful analysis of goals and objectives and some hypotheses about maximum arrangement of spatial components. Some basic dimensions which should be considered are whether the intent is to be open or closed, interactive or one-way, active or relatively passive, group or individually oriented, and independent or directed.

Student characteristics should be considered where possible. In order to accommodate a range of student characteristics as well as changes within individuals, it may be a good idea to offer a variety of learning spaces. In settings where information presentation is a major goal, spatial arrangement may not be critical. However, when interaction and highly active independent and group learning is sought, appropriate spatial configuration may be a key to success. Thus, space decisions should be related directly to instructional goals.

Decision-Making Information

The major source of information for making space decisions should be the instructional goals. Analyses of these goals should lead to some conclusions regarding optimal arrangement of space. There are additional sources which can lead to effective decisions; these are:

1. *Student Opinion.* Weinstein (1976) questioned students as to why they did not utilize some spaces. She found the girls found the science area "messy." This led her to propose the addition of shelving for storage of materials to make this area neater as well as to display the materials in a more palatable manner.

2. *Observation.* By observing space utilization patterns, much can be learned about the way students use space. Problems can be noted in terms of resource utilization which do not meet expectation, and subsequent revisions can be attempted to effect changes in the use of space. This observation should include the quantity as well as the quality of utilization.

3. *Student Background.* Students' past experience and achievement can lead to some tentative conclusions regarding space configuration. Students with a history of low achievement may need revised or special spaces to study and learn. Creative students may need more complex arrangements to allow for increased opportunities.

Summary

Conscious arrangement of instructional space, when this is in line with instructional goals, may be a powerful factor in the success of a learning program. It is not fully clear, however, what the relative importance of space arrangements may be. At this time, it appears that the major concern should be with arranging space to conform to instructional goals. It also appears that conscious decisions on spatial arrangement are more critical for instructional programs with goals that stress interaction, openness, and active learning.

References

Drew, C.J. Research on the Psychological-Behavioral Effect of the Physical Environment. *Review of Educational Research,* 1971, *41,* 447-465.

Knirk, F.G. *Designing Productive Learning Environments.* Englewood Cliffs, New Jersey: Educational Technology Publications, 1979.

Weinstein, C.S. The Effect of a Change in the Physical Design of an Open Classroom on Student Behavior. Paper presented at the meeting of the American Educational Research Association, San Francisco, California, 1976.

12

Grouping

The term grouping usually evokes thoughts of ability groups or homogeneous groups of students. This is a somewhat different idea than the purpose of this sub-component, grouping, in responsive instruction. This chapter will begin with a brief review of information on ability grouping and articulate how this contrasts with grouping in responsive instruction. This will be followed by some suggested grouping strategies and finally suggested procedures for acquiring decision-making information.

Ability Grouping

There is a relatively longstanding and widespread practice of grouping students in public education. There are a number of ways students may be grouped: by age, sex, intelligence test score, aptitude test scores, discipline categories, exceptionalities, etc. The number of actual as well as possible categories for grouping students together or separately is infinite. The most obvious category, in terms of frequency, for grouping students in school settings is age. The most controversial categories for grouping students in the United States are undoubtedly intelligence/aptitude and exceptionalities. Both categories appear to be relatively widely used throughout the United States. The majority of controversy centers around the notion of ability or homogeneous grouping.

Homogeneous grouping occurs when students are grouped together for instructional purposes because of similarity on one or more dimensions. Any dimension may be selected for grouping students. In practice, ability grouping involves use of only one or at most two dimensions based on scores from a standardized test. Several kinds of test scores are commonly used to group students, such as total score (an IQ measure of some sort), a sub-score (such as verbal IQ or reading readiness or achievement), or a combination of sub-scores (such as reading and arithmetic ability). At this point, it is sufficient to point out that these scores represent a small portion of the constellation of characteristics which constitute any human personality.

The rationale for ability grouping is relatively straightforward and deceptively sensible. If students of similar ability are grouped together, then the complexity of instruction is appreciably reduced. As a result, students may be given individual attention at least as far as learning rate is concerned, and appropriate learning materials. In addition, since all students are essentially similar, they will be more easily taught; students are more realistically challenged to do their best, and it is possible to give more precise individual attention to each student (Esposito, 1973). This is clearly not an unreasonable position and, conceptually, makes a good deal of sense.

When one looks at the research on ability grouping, however, it is apparent that what appears conceptually sound is not practically fruitful. Findlay and Bryan (1970), in an extensive review of ability grouping, concluded:

1. Ability grouping results in no overall achievement gains for students. In addition, middle- and low-ability students appear to suffer achievement deficits when grouped by ability.

2. Affective results from ability grouping are generally negative. High-ability students tend to get an over-inflated opinion of themselves, and average and below average groups must bear the stigma of being explicitly relegated to the lower orders of learning ability.

3. Ability grouping separates students into elitist and subordinate groups which, unfortunately, most often conform to socioeconomic and ethnic distinctions.

4. In studies where ability grouping resulted in favorable

outcomes, these appear to have been the result of curricular changes rather than the grouping strategy. That is, in most studies where results favorable to ability grouping were found when grouping was instituted, curricular changes were concurrently introduced.

Thus, there is little reason to believe that ability grouping produces any positive results for either student or teacher.

Let us examine some possible reasons for these findings. First, students are grouped ordinarily on only one or two dimensions. When more dimensions are included, grouping students becomes a very complex and tedious exercise. However, student differences occur on many dimensions; to group on the basis of one or two ignores the possible effects the myriad other dimensions may have on student learning. Some of these may be much more important than the dimension on which students were grouped. For example, students grouped on the basis of general intelligence scores may vary widely in terms of learning style and interest. Thus, their achievement may vary widely even though they remain similar on an intelligence measure.

Second, human beings are not homogeneous within themselves. That is, individuals invariably have peaks and valleys in achievement and aptitude profiles. A student who is average in terms of a total intelligence score may score fairly high on verbal abilities and quite low on quantitative abilities. To group all average score students together negates any advantage for such a student. He or she would be too advanced for verbally oriented work and behind for quantitative work. The effect, then, is that the total variability of the group has only been reduced by a small amount when students are grouped on one or two dimensions. And no reduction in intra-individual variability has been effected.

Other objections to ability grouping exist which are more philosophical. These include that ability grouping is antithetical to democracy, that ability grouping is a distortion of reality, and that ability grouping gives teachers a false sense of providing individualized attention. In addition, Kelly (1976) reported that there "appears to be a strong relationship between track (group) position and such outcomes as youth deviance" (p. 385). All may be valid objections depending upon your point of view. However, it appears to be clear that, regardless of philosophical beliefs, no advantage accrues to either students or teachers through homogeneous ability grouping. In addition, it also seems relatively clear that the majority of students are harmed either socially or academically by being grouped homogeneously by ability.

Rationale for Grouping

Although research evidence is unfavorable to homogeneous ability grouping, there are many other ways that students may be grouped. The ultimate goal in responsive instruction for grouping is to group students together in a way that will facilitate learning. To do this, students may work individually or in any size group from small to large, as well as for many different purposes. There are a number of sources of information a teacher might use to make grouping decisions. These range from relatively simple sources, such as individual student preferences, to quite complex sources, such as achievement scores on teacher-made tests. Decisions on grouping center around the issue of what type of grouping to use, the purposes for which students should be grouped, and how students should be selected into or out of groups.

Before dealing with these decision issues, one frequently referred to group-related issue should be discussed: group size. A good deal of research has been conducted on group size, particularly large versus small classes. We will not address the issue of whether large or small classes are better, because this appears to be an irrelevant question. Large or small, the size of a class should make no difference unless one believes that the number and proximity of human beings affect learning. The real issue here is what teachers do in large and small classes that result in quantitative or qualitative learning differences. These differences are the result of different instructional strategies rather than group size.

Our emphasis here will be on the purpose of the grouping strategy. In other words, we will look at reasons for forming students into groups and for disbanding groups. To be consistent with the approach of responsive instruction, groups should be formed for specific purposes—to aid student learning of specific skills, values, or knowledge—and, once these purposes are met, the groups should ordinarily be disbanded or reformed.

Grouping Strategies

Let's begin by looking at some advantages for heterogeneous grouping. Here, heterogeneous grouping can be considered in two ways. First, students can be grouped randomly. Ordinarily, such grouping will be done within some constraints, such as age. That is, all students of a similar age or grade level are randomly placed in groups of a specified size. Second, students may be specifically placed in one or another group in order to maximize individual differences. The latter approach is relatively difficult to accomplish without the identification of a specific student-related need. However, students could be specifically heterogeneously grouped on dimensions such as cultural background, ability, or interests. One advantage of such an approach would be to allow students to have contact with others who are different from themselves.

There is some research which indicates that heterogeneously grouped students profit from being with others different from themselves. For example, Brown and Wunderlich (1976) concluded, "Students in these settings (heterogeneous groups) were more satisfied, experienced less friction, and felt more cohesiveness in the classroom than did those in ability-grouped settings" (p. 7). Thompson (1974) concluded that his evidence "strongly suggests that heterogeneous grouping does the greatest good for the greatest number of students when achievement gain is the measure for learning in 11th grade American History" (p. 78). Thompson goes on to warn that "one cannot claim that heterogeneous grouping is universally better for all students," since some students in homogeneously grouped classes did better than some in heterogeneously grouped classes. The evidence, thus, leads in the same direction as most research on other instructional variables. That is, there is no clear-cut advantage for all individual students with any grouping strategy. As individuals, students will respond differentially to grouping. Some prosper under one style, while others prosper under a different style. The decision about grouping, then, must be based on student needs and must be responsive to those needs.

One clear advantage of forming instructional groups with a mix of student characteristics is that students have an opportunity to compare and model other students' performance. This is particularly advantageous for low-ability students since, if they are always grouped with low-ability students, they may never see or experience high-quality work. However, if grouped with high-ability students, they can see and attempt to model the performance of more able students.

In any event, the purpose for grouping students must be clearly thought out so that greater student achievement results. It is unlikely, based on the research reviewed and rationale presented, that any single grouping strategy will be meritorious for all students. It is equally unlikely that any single grouping will be best for any single student across the total curriculum. Our only conclusion, then, is that grouping must be done for special purposes (e.g., Hamilton, 1960) in order to maximize the benefits of differential grouping.

Special Purpose Grouping

We will now review several grouping strategies and identify some of the purposes for such strategies.

Special Need Grouping. This approach is labeled in various ways such as "Flexible Skill Grouping" (Wilson and Ribovich, 1973). The intent is to form students into temporary groups because of some special skill the students possess or because they all have a particular weakness. For these groups, special instructional programs can be developed for the students involved which address or take advantage of their deficit or ability. The purpose of grouping students would be to supply instruction related to the identified student needs. This could involve enrichment experiences as well as remedial work. Once the special need is obviated, then the group would be disbanded.

Teacher decisions about forming and disbanding special need groups could be based on several sources of information. Achievement on teacher-made tests could be one such source. Another, broader approach, could be to identify students who would profit from development of specific abilities, such as creativity or critical thinking. Information to make such grouping decisions could come from teacher observations, past achievement records, or scores on standardized tests measuring these competencies.

Interest Grouping. Students may be grouped on the basis of particular interests related to content. For example, students interested in one aspect of the content could be grouped together to pursue that interest in depth. Ordinarily, this would involve in-depth study of a general topic. If the legislative process of a democracy were being studied, for example, one group might study election procedures, another might study how deliberations are conducted among legislators, while another might compare different governmental styles.

Decisions relative to interest grouping ordinarily would be left to students. It is quite important, however, that the areas be carefully selected to conform with varying student interests. Decisions about what interest areas to choose may be made by asking students, choosing among carefully selected topic areas, or by focusing on topics about which students frequently ask questions. These data may be gathered through observation or by questioning students.

Free Choice Grouping. This type of grouping is most appropriate when a number of alternatives are offered to students. They may then choose among the alternatives those which they like best. Group choices may be differentiated by levels of difficulty, interests, activities, or any other relevant dimension. The important notion is to give students a real choice so there should be some purposeful contrast between activities. Choice can be completely free or controlled. That is, students may be allowed to enter groups at will or be required to conform to some pattern of membership. For example, students could be required to attend at least three different groups per week. This would force students to experience some variety and not get fixed at one level or interest.

Development of free choice groups should be based on student needs as determined by assessment data. Thus, the dimensions upon which the groups will be developed should be based on identified needs. If a wide variance in ability is present, different levels of material might be the best approach. If differences are great in socioeconomic backgrounds, cultural experiences might serve as a useful basis for orienting group structure. The alternatives are endless. Of course, groups may be structured on more than one dimension, such as cultural experiences and interests. Decision data may be gathered from the full range of assessment data available, special questionnaires, and curricular analyses.

Peer Grouping. Peer grouping is an approach which has been fairly widely researched and written about in recent years (e.g., Hassinger and Via, 1969; Stainback, Stainback, and Lichtward, 1975). From a grouping point of view, the objective is to place two or more students together in a way that they may enhance each other's learning. The relevant dimensions for decision-making are which and how many students should be working together. There are many possibilities. Students may be allowed to choose their own co-worker(s), be grouped on interest or ability, or be placed in large or small groups. There are several criteria which should be met if such groups are to be successful. First, there must be a specific purpose for the group. Second, the students must know how to work together and productively in groups. Third, the students must understand their responsibilities within the group.

Decisions on what kind of peer groups to establish, when, and for what purpose should again rest on student and curricular needs. If some students, for example, are particularly skilled in an area under study, they may serve as tutors to either individuals or groups of students. Data for decision-making can be drawn from assessment data, student questionnaires, and observation.

Large/Small Groups. As stated earlier, there is little reason to believe that group size will have any effect on learning. However, it is clear that group size may have an effect on the success of some instructional strategies. Large groups are not good for discussion sessions, and small groups are not advantageous if students must just sit and listen. Therefore, decisions about whether to form large or small groups should be based on the type of instructional strategy to be used as well as student needs. In most cases, such grouping decisions will be secondary to decisions made on strategies. (For a comprehensive discussion of small groups, see Sharan and Sharan, 1976.)

Decision-Making Data

The following procedures may be used to gather data for making grouping decisions.

1. *Questionnaires.* Questions on questionnaires for grouping decisions should be oriented to discovering, first, some relevant dimensions for grouping (i.e., interests, abilities, etc.), and second, how the students react to these dimensions (i.e., what are their interests, etc.). This may require two separate questionnaires and, from time to time, repeat questionnaires.

2. *Observation.* The focus of observation can be on such dimensions as expressed student interests, social patterns, special abilities, curricular interests, and so forth. These observations may be used to tentatively identify questionnaire items or for more structured observation.

3. *Aptitude/Intelligence Tests.* These tests may be used to make tentative decisions relative to the basic structure of the group. From standardized profiles, you can begin to determine the amount of variability that exists in the group on ability, interests, aptitudes, etc. These data may then be used to further specify decisions about grouping based on questionnaire and observation data.

4. *Teacher-Made Achievement Tests.* When achievement is related to well-specified objectives, these objectives may serve as useful forms for grouping, particularly for remedial grouping. This can be done by noting response patterns of students; those students who consistently make errors on objectives directly related to each other may be grouped together if the problem stems from the same source.

Summary

Grouping refers to the way in which students are brought together when learning. Students may work/study individually or in any combination of numbers to form a group. The purpose for grouping students together is to meet particular learning needs. Students should only be grouped for specific purposes on the basis of specific information. General grouping strategies, such as homogeneous ability grouping, do not appear to be advantageous for either students or teachers. However, grouping students together for specific needs is an economical and useful way to aid student learning.

References

Brown, S.W., and Wunderlich, K.W. The Effect of Open Concept Education and Ability Grouping on Achievement Level Concerning the Teaching of Fifth Grade Mathematics. Paper presented at the meeting of the American Educational Research Association, San Francisco, 1976.

Esposito, D. Homogeneous and Heterogeneous Ability Grouping: Principal Findings and Implications for Evaluating and Designing More Effective Educational Environments. *Review of Educational Research,* 1973, *43,* 163-179.

Findlay, W.C., and Bryan, M.M. *Ability Grouping: 1970, Status Impact and Alternatives.* Center for Educational Improvement, University of Georgia, Athens, Georgia, 1970.

Hamilton, N.K. Providing for Individual Differences. *Educational Leadership,* 1960, *18,* 177-182.

Hassinger, J., and Via, M. How Much Does a Tutor Learn Through Teaching Reading? *Journal of Secondary Education,* 1969, *44,* 42-44.

Kelly, D.H. Track Position, School Misconduct, and Youth Deviance. *Urban Education,* 1976, *10,* 379-388.

Sharan, S., and Sharan, Y. *Small-Group Teaching.* Englewood Cliffs, New Jersey: Educational Technology Publications, 1976.

Stainback, W.C., Stainback, W.C., and Lichtward, F. The Research Evidence Regarding the Student-to-Student Tutoring Approach to Individualized Instruction. *Educational Technology,* February, 1975.

Thompson, G.W. The Effects of Ability Grouping Upon Achievement in Eleventh Grade American History. *The Journal of Experimental Education,* 1974, *22,* 76-79.

Wilson, R.M., and Ribovich, J.K. Ability Grouping? Stop and Reconsider. *Reading World,* 1973, *13,* 84-91.

Part V: Evaluation

13

Evaluation

With the rise of calls for accountability in education, evaluation has become a major activity throughout organized education. This has spawned a vast amount of writing about evaluation as well as publication of a multitude of evaluation studies. As with many burgeoning fields, the output is almost overwhelming and often confusing. We will try to provide some perspective on evaluation so that the role evaluation plays in instructional design becomes clear.

The major purpose of evaluation activities is to provide data on which decisions can be based. First, let us make clear that evaluation, as distinguished from assessment, is an "after-the-fact" activity. That is, evaluation data are gathered after a program or portion of a program has been completed. This does not mean that evaluation should be considered only following implementation of a complete instructional program. Quite the contrary, evaluation activities must be planned prior to implementation *as an integral part of the total instructional design.* Evaluation activities interact with all other components of instruction and, like all other components, must be responsive to student needs.

What is evaluation? Essentially, evaluation is comparing actual outcomes with intended outcomes. To do so requires that intended outcomes be well-formulated and that data be made available to indicate if the intended outcomes are met. Evaluation is not decision-making; decisions are made on the basis of the evaluation activities. That is, once it is established how closely actual outcomes match intended outcomes, the decision-maker uses this information to make decisions. Thus, evaluation is basically the process of gathering decision-making information about success or failure. We will examine the nature of these decisions in some detail later, in the sections on programmatic evaluation and individual student evaluation. The rest of this section will be devoted to defining some concepts which are important for understanding, planning, and conducting evaluation.

Norm-Referenced. Norm-referenced evaluation is a comparative referencing of performance to a standard based on the test behavior of many comparable individuals. In other words, a standard or norm is established based on the composite scores of many individuals. This standard or norm is then used to interpret the performance of subsequent testees. By referring to the "norm," all individual scores can be ranked on a relative scale such that it is possible to tell the relative standing of each individual (i.e., 20th, 30th, 50th, 80th percentile) compared with all other individuals who have taken the test. Data from norm-referenced tests are useful *only* if there is a wide spread of scores. Without such variability, it would be impossible to order scores in a relative and useful way. Since this variability is essential for comparative judgments, test makers must write tests very carefully in order to achieve it. Generally, test items are added, subtracted, and modified until sufficient variability of performance is achieved.

Norm-referenced tests generally measure relatively global abilities in a comprehensive way. The abilities may be very general, such as IQ, or less general, such as verbal abilities or reading readiness. In most cases, however, the results allow for judgments relative to the development of general abilities, with little notion of the contribution of any specific abilities relating to the general abilities. As a result, norm-referenced tests rarely can be used effectively for diagnostic purposes. Norm-referenced tests also sample the knowledge of respondents. There is, then, an element of chance involved; the test items may coincide with the domain of knowledge held by an individual, or they may not. If they do not, the test score will be low and won't represent the individual's true level of knowledge. This presents particular problems for individuals who are quite different from the norm group, since their scores are likely to be somewhat lower.

Norm-referenced tests are often thought to be indicators of ability. This appears to be particularly true for instruments which yield IQ type scores. It should be noted that ability (i.e., intellectual ability or ability to learn) is not reflected directly in such scores. These scores represent the amount of information the respondent has learned which is included in the instrument. Further, the score may be lower (but never higher) than it actually is, due to testing conditions and motivational factors. The individual abilities and talents possessed by an individual usually do not show up on such tests—only general abilities.

What are the uses of such scores? Program comparison is one use. Also, it is true that students with higher scores tend to do much better in school than students with lower scores. Thus, one purpose for utilization of these scores may be to identify students who have not profited greatly from instruction received in the past. Other uses for these instruments have been indicated in previous chapters.

A final note on norm-referenced tests: They are very difficult to develop and require a great deal of time and technical expertise to prepare. This includes statistical expertise to item-analyze test items and the resources to field test and norm the test.

Criterion-Referenced. "A criterion-referenced test is used to ascertain an individual's status with respect to a well-defined behavior domain" (Popham, 1975, p. 130). The relative standing of individuals is irrelevant with criterion-referenced tests. The purpose of this form of evaluation is to determine how close an individual is to a specific criterion or set of criteria. Thus, the notion of relativity is not at issue; instead the mastery of content related goals is emphasized. Popham used the term "well-defined behavior domain," which may be somewhat confusing. He is referring to a specification of a class of behaviors rather than specifying an infinite number of highly specific outcomes. An example of the difference here would be between an outcome such as "demonstrate correct use of adjectives" and "use the word blue correctly," "use the word high correctly," "use the word tight correctly," and so forth. The focus on domains results in a much more economical and practical approach to evaluation.

We looked at criteria specification in the chapter on objectives. We will not belabor the necessity for specifying criteria here. However, it is important to note that if criteria are well-established, evaluation is made considerably easier for criterion-referenced evaluation.

Criterion-referenced evaluation is particularly useful for determining the progress individuals make toward meeting learning goals. Group comparisons are not so easily made, since the point of reference is to an absolute criterion rather than to relative standards. When criteria are established, the relative standing of individuals is not a necessary consideration, since everyone can be compared against the criteria. In other words, performance is judged against the criteria rather than against the performance of other students.

Reliability. This term was defined in the chapter on assessment in terms of the amount of confidence which can be placed in the source of information. For evaluation instruments, this may be rephrased as how well or with what consistency a test measures what it is supposed to measure. No matter how many times the instrument is used, the results should be about the same. If you think of a yardstick, when measuring the length of an object, the yardstick should not vary, and thus it should yield the same measure each time. This would be a very reliable instrument. If the yardstick were made of elastic, it would be considerably less reliable than if made of metal. An evaluation instrument should operate the same as a metal yardstick, yielding the same measure each time it is used. There are a number of ways to establish reliability of test instruments; these methods are discussed in numerous texts on evaluation, and you should refer to one of these for detail on this point. Citations for several such texts are listed in the Reference section of this chapter.

Validity. Validity of a test indicates whether the test instrument measures what it is supposed to measure. Three types of validity are most commonly referred to: content validity, criterion-related validity, and construct validity (APA, 1974). The validity of a test relates directly to how well future performance can be predicted on the basis of present test performance. The American Psychological Association (APA, 1974) described criterion-related validity (predictive and concurrent) as applying "when one wishes to infer from a test score an individual's most probable standing on some other variable called a criterion" (p. 26). The APA pointed out the distinction between predictive and concurrent validity as one (concurrent) indicating the *status quo* or where the individual is now and the other (predictive) indicating where the individual will be following the passage of time (ordinarily, this includes some training program). This distinction is important depending on the use to which the test will be put.

Content validity "is required when the test user wishes to estimate how an individual performs in the universe of situations the test is intended to represent" (APA, 1974, p. 28). In other words, the test must be representative of what it is intended for the learner to learn. This requires a definition of the performance domain covered in the test, and predictions based on test results are applicable only to this domain.

Construct validity refers to how well the test measures the presence or absence of a "construct." Constructs are ordinarily hypothetical, psychological traits or states, such as anxiety and reading readiness. These constructs cannot be readily observed but often are the result of many interrelated psychological and personality dimensions. To establish construct validity, the test maker must posit a hypothesis which will account for test performance and then test this hypothesis against results on the test.

Test validity, like reliability, is a relatively technical concept which is also ordinarily covered in texts on educational measurement. The texts cited in the Reference section can supply the needed background for those not familiar with these terms. It will suffice to say here that validity is an important concept for all tests and should be carefully considered. Tests which are not reliable cannot be valid, since they would possess no consistency. However, a test may be reliable and still not be valid. The reliability and validity of all published tests should be documented in the test manuals. A review of reliability and validity data can aid the instructional developer in the selection of appropriate test instruments. The criterion for appropriateness is, generally, whether or not the test meets the specific purposes the decision-maker has for the instrument.

Summative Evaluation. According to Bloom, Hastings, and Madaus (1971), summative evaluation is distinguished from formative evaluation on three dimensions: purpose, time, and level of generalization. Summative evaluation "is directed toward a much more general assessment of the degree to which the larger outcomes have been attained over the entire course (experience) or some substantial part of it" (Bloom, Hastings, and Madaus, 1971, p. 61). The purpose is to make generalizations relative to goals and future actions. The time included is substantial or of larger units of instruction, and generalizations would tend toward statements relative to conceptual development or overall skill acquisition. An example of summative evaluation would be a final exam in a history course which seeks to acquire data relative to students' development of factual information as well as abilities to problem-solve and utilize historical methodology. The goal is to evaluate learning over a long-term experience (a course) and to make generalizations of the sort that students can problem-solve and know how to use the historical method effectively. On the basis of such a test, it should be possible to predict how well students might use problem-solving skills and historical methodology in future situations.

Formative Evaluation. In contrast to summative evaluation, which occurs after the learning has taken place, formative evaluation is conducted while the learning is still in formation or during the learning program. The purpose is to acquire information to improve the ongoing learning; the time included is of short duration (i.e., a lesson or short unit); and generalizations are limited to the specific content of the lesson or unit involved. The goal of formative evaluation is to gather data which will result in instructional improvement and, thus, improve the probability of learning.

The efficacy of formative evaluation can be shown in the following explanation. Most instruction is developed sequentially such that preceding concepts are necessary for subsequent learning. If a student misses the primary concepts, he or she is likely to have difficulty with subsequent requirements. If these failures can be detected and corrected early, then the probability of learning is increased. This evaluation of learning-in-formation can increase the overall efficiency and effectiveness of a learning program.

Summative and formative evaluation are essential to developing a complete understanding of both program effects and individual student learning. Sherman and Winstead (1975) have pointed out that instruction is made up of many instructional sessions, each of which contribute to overall student development. In order to understand the impact of each session on total development, formative evaluation must be used. However, many instructional programs have general goals which require synthesis of individual learning objectives into more global abilities; this represents an intention for the whole to be greater than the sum of the parts, to borrow Gestaltist language. This can only be evaluated using summative evaluation.

We will now incorporate this terminology into programmatic and individual student evaluation.

Programmatic Evaluation

A major concern for all instructional developers is whether the instruction developed is any good. If it is good, then it must be determined how good and where it should be revised. To provide answers to questions about the quality of an instructional program, the developer must evaluate the program relative to goals established for the program. In responsive instruction, an additional issue must be dealt with relative to how responsive the program is to individual student needs. The goal of these evaluation efforts is to provide data for making decisions about the instruction.

Programmatic evaluation must be conducted systematically. That is, an integral part of the instructional design must be program evaluation. Basically, this involves four categories of decisions: to no longer use the program; to revise the program; to restrict the program; or to redevelop the program. The planning of instruction should include data-gathering which will result in sufficient information to make a decision in one of these categories.

The basic issue here is one of instructional quality; the following approach to determining instructional quality is based on a model presented by Sherman (1977). This model includes three basic evaluation categories: Instructional Development, Delivery, and Student Achievement (see Figure 13.1). The approach is consistent with the responsive instruction model in that instruction is conceived as a multi-dimensional enterprise which requires data from a broad range of categories to provide decision-making data about the program. Once these data are gathered, the instructional developer has information to make decisions on the status of the program.

The first evaluation category, moving up from the bottom of the chart, is instructional development. The focus here is on the planning in which the developer engages during instructional development. The rationale for this is based on the notion presented earlier that conscious, rational decisions are more appropriate for instructional development than decisions which are arrived at by other means. Thus, the first step in programmatic evaluation is to examine the planning process. The three categories of information stressed throughout this book are used as the focus for evaluating planning decisions. That is, all decisions should be based on empirical data, assessment data, and logic. The evaluation task in this category is two-fold.

First, the conscious decisions made by the developer must be identified. For responsive instruction, these decisions center around all the components of this book's instructional model. Second, the process involves systematically reviewing each decision in the instructional components and asking the following questions: (1) Was the available empirical evidence used in making instructional decisions? (2) Were assessment data employed to make instructional decisions? (3) What is the logic behind each decision?

There are no standards for determining what planning should be considered meritorious and what should be considered lacking. The resulting data must be judged in light of the quantity and

Figure 13.1

Evaluation Categories and Evaluation Activities
Employed in Evaluating the Quality of Instruction
(adapted from Sherman, 1977)

Evaluation Categories	Evaluation Activities
Student Achievement	A. Learning Referenced to Goals B. Learning Referenced to Norms
Delivery	A. Formative B. Summative

Instructional Development	A. Identify Planning Decisions
	B. Review Decisions
	    1. Empirical Data
	    2. Assessment Data
	    3. Logic

quality of information used in making instructional decisions. The data available vary from component to component, and it is also possible that a developer might choose to ignore specific decisions on one or more components of the responsive instruction model. The result of this sort of evaluation should yield a judgment on how well the instruction was planned. Such data can be valuable in making decisions on the status of an instructional program.

For example, if a program is judged to be a failure and data are available which indicate the instruction was poorly planned, then larger decisions about the efficacy of the concept underlying the instruction must be delayed. It could be that a well-conceived instructional idea would be unsuccessful when put into practice, due to poor planning. This, incidentally, is often the case in situations where innovations are implemented and fail. Failure is almost guaranteed by poor planning and lack of understanding on the part of those implementing the innovation. Thus, rather than abandon concepts such as "open schools," "behavior modification," or "core curriculum," emphasis should be placed on the planning process used to put the concept into practice. If the planning is wanting, then little can be said about the innovative concept.

The second component is delivery. The concern here is with how well the instructional program was implemented and received. The focus is on consumer or student evaluation. The majority of research on student evaluation has been done in higher education (see Costin, Greenough, and Menges, 1971; Kulik and McKeachie, 1975; and Sherman, 1975), and the majority of this research is on summative or course-end evaluation. There is little evidence which supports the use of this approach as a good way alone to judge the quality of instruction. However, consumer evaluation does provide one category of data which can be useful in developing an overall evaluation of instructional quality.

Two forms of consumer evaluation are recommended: formative and summative. Formative evaluation should focus on student evaluation of basic units of an instructional program. These may be lessons, small units, packages, or some other organizational unit. Sherman and Winstead (1975) have described one way in which formative evaluation by students may be implemented. This involved students rating each lesson at the end of each lesson using a five-point Likert-type scale. The authors claimed these ratings gave the instructor an idea of the relative contribution of each lesson to the overall judgment of quality given to the course. Lessons which were inferior could be identified and modified, and good lessons could be retained and improved. The idea of formative evaluation appears to be one that should be incorporated into an evaluation plan.

The second form of consumer evaluation is summative evaluation. There is a good deal of controversy over what kind of summative evaluation is best. Most course-end evaluations are rather general in nature and yield nonspecific data. This is not surprising, since a global judgment is requested.

The rationale for summative course evaluation is to gather global impressions from students. These global impressions may conform with formative evaluations or be somewhat different. It appears that the best way to gather summative impressions from students is to seek nonspecific judgments. These may be gathered in the form of overall ratings, such as "What grade would you give the instructor?," or may be in narrative form in response to questions, such as "What did you like best and least about the course?" These judgments, when considered in conjunction with formative data, should give a fairly accurate picture of the general and specific qualities of the instruction being evaluated.

Student achievement is the third component of programmatic evaluation. Here we are concerned with the general level of student learning rather than individual achievement. That is, we are interested in the general level of achievement or learning reached by students in the instructional program. This is an important issue, since a program may be very effective when considered in isolation. That is, students could learn all that is taught, but what is taught might not be adequate for their present or future needs. Thus, we need to consider two aspects of student learning: learning compared to instructional goals and learning compared to expectations for similar instructional experiences.

Relative to the first aspect, student learning should be compared to instructional goals. Data to judge this come from a compilation of student learning by summing across all students. There are a number of ways to do this. We will give two examples, but the best procedure may vary, depending upon the nature of the instruction. Student achievement may be grouped into percentages achieving different proportions of objectives or goals. That is, 60 percent of the group achieved 100 percent of the objectives, 20 percent achieved between 90 percent and 99 percent, ten percent achieved between 80 percent and 89 percent, etc. Achievement summaries may also be computed on the basis of time, indicating that 40 percent achieved 100 percent of the objectives in two weeks, 40 percent achieved 100 percent in four weeks, and so forth. The decision should be based on the relevant dimensions for the instruction. This is obviously a planning decision which must be made during the initial planning of the instruction.

The second aspect of evaluating learning involves comparing learners in the instruction with learners in other, similar instructional experiences. For example, students in high school biology are expected to learn a certain amount of biology. The only way to determine if students are achieving at a rate which is equal to expectations is to compare the level of achievement of the group in the evaluated instruction with the general expectation. Again, there are several ways this can be done. One is to compare a group composite score with a norm on a standardized instrument. This is frequently done with reading scores in elementary education; the composite reading level of a school or district is compared against the norms for the instrument. Other ways to gain comparative data of this sort are to compare numbers of Merit scholars versus number expected and numbers produced in past years, and to see how students perform in content related competitions across schools or districts, such as in science fairs and essay contests.

There is one relatively major problem with interpretation of grouped score comparisons of this sort. There is a general feeling among educators that being at or below the mean is distasteful. However, it is impossible obviously for everyone to be above average and for every program to be above average. This is not to say that excellence shouldn't be pursued relentlessly. It is to say that comparative data should be interpreted carefully and realistically. These data must be considered in light of the context from which they come. Students may be expected to achieve at higher or lower levels than the norm, depending on situational differences. In some cases, instructional gains may be claimed if students achieve at the norm but in less time.

An accurate picture of student achievement can be determined only if both composite learning and comparative learning are considered. Data from both sources can lead to more accurate decisions about the status of an instructional program relative to the need for abandonment, revision, restriction, or redevelopment.

No program can be accurately evaluated for effectiveness, unless all three components—planning, presenting, and student achievement—are considered. The instructional decision-maker must have sufficient and comprehensive information to make judgments about the quality of the instruction, just as he or she must have good information to make decisions regarding each separate component of the responsive instruction model. It is clear that these decision data will not be available unless specifically planned during the development of instruction. This is why the notion of evaluation of the quality of instruction is included as part of the evaluation component.

Individual Student Evaluation

Evaluation of student learning is conducted for three purposes: to determine if students have learned, to provide data for checking on the quality of instruction, and to diagnose errors for remediation. We have discussed the second purpose earlier in this chapter and will deal extensively with the third purpose in the next chapter. Our major focus here will be on the determination of student learning.

Let's begin with a brief discussion of why student learning must be evaluated. Clearly, the purpose is to see if and what students have learned. The primary purpose of evaluation is not to give grades or to motivate students to learn, although these may be legitimate secondary purposes. Determining what students learn also implies the ability to determine what they have *not* learned. We must be able to pinpoint what students have and haven't learned.

Evaluation of student learning is tied closely to instructional objectives. The relationship is so close and interactive that some instructional designers recommend that evaluation procedures be developed before objectives (e.g., Davis, Alexander, and Yelon, 1974). Basically, evaluation must be directly aimed at objectives, since if an objective or goal is important enough to be stated, student learning should be evaluated relative to it. We are not recommending a sampling approach where small portions of student learning are sampled in order to infer the general level of learning. A sampling approach does not allow either for specificity or comprehensiveness. When every objective is evaluated, the instructor can develop a clear picture of achievement measured against what was planned for students to learn.

Instruction must be evaluated relative to both goals and objectives. Goals usually provide organization for large units incorporating many objectives. Objectives, while generally related, ordinarily do not subsume learning included in other objectives. As a result, objectives may be evaluated without concern for previous objectives or subsequent objectives, since objectives represent relatively small amounts of learning. Goals, on the other hand, represent large units of learning which include both specific and general components. Thus, it seems reasonable to approach the evaluation of goals and objectives differently. We will discuss evaluating learning associated with objectives first and follow this with evaluation of learning associated with goals.

Evaluation of Learning Associated with Objectives. Objectives represent relatively small amounts of learning immediately associated with instruction. That is, objectives specify what students are to be able to do as a result of the instruction presented at a specific time. It follows that evaluation of learning associated with objectives be relatively immediate in order to determine if students are able to meet the objectives of a particular instructional session. It also follows that this evaluation should be utilized to aid students who do not master the objectives. This is essentially a criterion-referenced approach to formative evaluation.

There are several implications of this approach. First, students should be given relatively immediate feedback on their learning related to each objective. This is helpful to both students and teachers, since students are given a clear picture of their progress and teachers can make relatively immediate decisions regarding needed remediation to encourage and facilitate mastery. Thus, the evaluation data are used formatively to promote success and to avoid having students fall behind. Second, evaluation becomes an integral part of the instructional program. Teaching does not stop in order to determine if students have learned. There should be a steady rate of achievement as opposed to the flurry of study activity in which students often engage at examination time. Third, both teachers and students become accustomed to utilizing evaluation data to promote learning. Evaluation of objectives should be conducted frequently and be used to facilitate learning rather than to impose penalties for lack of learning.

Formative evaluation is ordinarily relatively informal, though quite specific. There are many ways to implement this type of evaluation; the decision rests on the nature of the content, the attributes/aptitudes of learners, and convenience. For example, brief evaluation exercises can be embedded in learning materials; review questions can be frequently posed; students can be given frequent simulation exercises; students can be required to do self-evaluation; and so forth. It is critical that formative evaluation be well-planned in order that some data are made apparent to the evaluator on a regular basis. This is not tantamount to asking a whole class, "Does everybody understand?" In most cases, such inquiries get no negative response, if any response at all.

The regularity of formative evaluation is another decision that must conform to student characteristics, content, and other factors. In general, neophyte students need more frequent evaluation than sophisticated students. Anxious students need more frequent evaluation, as do students who have lower perceptions of internal control or high needs for social approval. However, very frequent evaluation can sometimes get in the way of learning, in that students know they are correct and do not need to be told so. There is currently a good bit of controversy over the reinforcing properties of feedback, particularly knowledge of being correct. Frequently being told you are correct over small trials generally does not appear to facilitate learning. Feedback in such instances is most helpful when errors are indicated and information on how the errors can be corrected is included. However, frequent feedback does not seem to inhibit learning, though it can generate some frustration due to the delay in getting through material associated with it.

Decisions regarding the best procedure to use for a particular instructional program must be based on the nature of the instruction and learner needs. Both student and teacher need some security that the instruction is going well. In addition, it is certain that all students will not breeze through an instructional program with no problems. We must be able to identify problems as they arise. The only way to accomplish this is to implement formative evaluation. The unit of evaluation (lesson, module, unit, bi-weekly, etc.) is a matter for instructor decision based on content demands and learner needs. At a minimum, teachers should be able to intervene before students begin to experience serious problems. On the other hand, we do not want to make students totally dependent on outside evaluation for personal attribution of success. Obviously, this requires some careful planning and well-thought-out decisions.

It is probably a good idea to always include some student self-evaluation, which is criterion-referenced and formative. It is also wise to include some evaluation options so that students who require more frequent evaluation can receive it without difficulty. In other words, evaluation directed at objectives should be as flexible as possible, offering many opportunities to students as well as options for different ways to have their learning evaluated.

A final note on evaluation of learning associated with objectives: It may not be necessary for every student to master every objective. Sometimes it is easier to learn in retrospect in light of further learning than to master a specific objective or two initially. The basic purpose of this evaluation is to foster learning, so whatever activities accomplish this end are useful. Formative evaluation of this sort should not be used to determine grades but to establish a pattern of achievement which can be utilized to facilitate further learning. Objectives individually represent rather small pieces of the total goals for an instructional program. Mastery or failure to master each of the objectives does not accurately reflect achievement of the goals of the instructional program.

Evaluation of Learning Associated with Goals. The instructional goals represent the overall intended outcomes of instruction. In order to certify that students have achieved the outcomes, it is necessary to evaluate learning against goals. The purpose of most instruction is not to teach a series of isolated facts or skills but to develop in students a conceptual framework which can be generalized. It is these conceptual frameworks that goals specify.

We are faced with a two-part problem in evaluation of goal related learning. The first is to determine if the goal has been met. The second is to determine if the learning has been "taken" to the point that it is a relatively permanent part of the students' learning (or learned) repertoire.

The first task is to determine if students have mastered the instructional goals following the completion of the instruction. Doing this requires that a sufficient number of appropriate opportunities be made available to students to demonstrate their learning in a reliable way. What is sufficient and appropriate here constitutes the major instructional decisions for this evaluation task. Appropriateness relates to the validity of the evaluation items. In most cases, evaluation will be valid if it conforms to the intent of the goal as reflected in the objectives and subgoals included in the major goal. That is, the goal related evaluation should not require knowledge, skills, values, introduce conditions, etc., which do not appear as part of the instructional objectives. Novel material or conditions should not be sprung on students during evaluation. The teacher, then, can look for guidance in decision-making in the goals and objectives for making goal related evaluation appropriate or valid.

Sufficiency is another matter and somewhat more complex for the decision-maker. Since goals represent relatively broad learning outcomes, it is clear that one or two very specific questions will not serve as adequate evaluation. It is often the case that the major goals represent more than the combination of all objectives; this synthesis must be evaluated. Decisions on how this is done must be based on the goals involved and the nature of learning sought.

Evaluation of goal related learning is summative evaluation, since the intent is to evaluate large learning units, to certify mastery, and to generalize across time and situations. Therefore, the evaluation items should be broadly framed in order to incorporate all the learning subsumed in the instructional program. There should also be enough items so that the student has sufficient opportunities to demonstrate mastery and does not have a total score resting on performance on one or two answers.

Thus far, no attempt has been made to deal with the technological aspects of classroom evaluation. This is not accidental; the various advantages, disadvantages, and construction techniques associated with different testing formats are well-documented elsewhere (e.g., Hills, 1976). We will not replicate this information here. We will include here only a reminder that there are many formats which are used traditionally (e.g., multiple-choice, true-false, essay, etc.), as well as others which are used less frequently, such as products and performances. The decision on format should be consistent with the learning involved. Our goal here is to delineate the conceptual properties which summative goal related learning evaluation should possess in order to provide a decision-making framework for selection of evaluation procedures.

To further specify these properties, it is essential that although the evaluation is summative in nature, it should still be criterion-referenced. That is, the evaluation must be aimed at the specific learning goals contained in the goal statements. The purpose is to determine how student learning compares with goals. It is not the purpose to see which students have learned the most, as would be the case with a norm-referenced approach. The norming process is quite complex, demands large populations, and rarely yields data specific to absolute goal attainment. It is necessary, then, to establish absolutes for goals against which student learning can be compared in order for evaluation to be criterion-referenced.

The establishment of goal related absolutes is accomplished by constructing model responses which conform to goal statements. Ordinarily, these model responses would not be shared with students prior to the evaluation. It is important that these model responses reflect the intent of the goal. For example, if a process (cognitive strategy) is being taught, then the model response should be oriented to the process rather than the product of the response. If, on the other hand, synthesis of knowledge is represented in the goal, the response should be constructed in terms of the critical aspects of this synthesis. The end-result of these decisions should be a set of evaluation activities which are defensible as true indicators of student learning as well as providing sufficient data to certify that the student has mastered the learning or the degree to which the learning has been mastered.

The second part of goal related evaluation of learning is to determine if the learning has "taken" over time, or endured. Our purpose here is to see if the content learned is retained sufficiently to serve as a contribution to the students' general fund of knowledge. This requires post-instruction evaluation, or evaluation following the passage of time. Evaluation of this sort should be conducted in line with the stated intentions of the instruction. That is, it should be referenced to the place of the instruction in the overall plan of education. As such, the specific evaluation items should be of a general nature and designed to evaluate the long-term impact of the instruction on students.

Two aspects of learning may be evaluated: retention of specific learning and retention of more global learning. The actual evaluation instrument should be referenced to goal related criteria. Such evaluation may appear more similar to a survey than a test, including items such as, "What were the most helpful things you learned and why?"; "What were the least helpful and why?"; "How could the instruction have been improved?"; "What do you recall as the most important thing you learned?"; and so forth. Questions such as these will give the instructional decision-maker the benefit of the students' retrospect on the instruction. These data should provide information for making decisions relative to improving the relevance of the instruction as well as identify weak points.

Philosophy of Evaluation

Little evidence is available on the differential effects of various approaches to evaluation. The approach you take should be consistent with the content demands and your own beliefs about the purpose of evaluation. In responsive instruction, evaluation serves the purpose of promoting learning by providing data which can be used to make instructional procedures more responsive to students. This occurs on two levels. On a general level, an attempt is made to evaluate the quality of the instruction to insure that the instruction is as good as it can be. On a specific level, individual student achievement is addressed to insure that students are profiting to the maximum from the instruction.

Every effort should be made to insure that the evaluation procedures decided upon will, in fact, reflect what students have learned. It is of almost no benefit to know that one student is better than another, or that one student has learned an indefinably larger amount than another. It is helpful to know how students relate to specific criteria, since this gives an indication not only of what has been learned but also of what students still need to achieve.

Our discussion of evaluation has been rather general. We have prescribed no procedural guidelines but have offered a framework of criteria to which good instructional evaluation should conform. Evaluation must be developed through decisions related to these criteria. Hopefully, this will generate a philosophy of evaluation which will serve the instructional decision-maker better than specific guidelines.

To facilitate evaluation decisions, the following questions are suggested as a guide to developing evaluation procedures. These questions are organized around the basic elements of the evaluation component and are meant to guide, but not dictate, evaluation decisions.

I. *Evaluation of the Quality of Instruction*
   A. Are data gathered on instructional planning?
   B. Are data gathered on and from students on a formative and summative basis?
   C. Are student achievement data gathered on criterion-referenced and norm-referenced learning?

II. *Evaluation of Student Learning*
   A. Objectives related learning
      1. Are criterion-referenced data gathered?
      2. Can the data be used formatively?
      3. Are the data valid?
      4. Are the data reliable?
      5. Are data gathered frequently enough?
      6. Are the evaluation procedures practical and manageable?

B. Goal related learning
1. Are criterion-referenced data gathered?
2. Are the data valid?
3. Are students given sufficient opportunities to demonstrate their learning?
4. Are the data sufficient to certify learning?
5. Do the data reflect the intent of the goal statements?
6. Are follow-up data planned?
7. Do follow-up data reflect the long-term impact of the instruction?

Summary

Evaluation is the component of the responsive instruction model concerned with the results of the instructional program. Two categories of effects or results are examined: instructional quality and student learning. In both cases, the purpose for gathering evaluation data is to enable the decision-maker to make judgments about the instruction.

References

American Psychological Association. *Standards for Educational and Psychological Tests.* Washington, D.C.: American Psychological Association, Inc., 1974.

Bloom, B.S., Hastings, J.T., and Madaus, G.F. *Handbook on Formative and Summative Evaluation of Student Learning.* New York: McGraw-Hill, 1971.

Costin, F., Greenough, W.T., and Menges, R.J. Student Ratings of College Teaching: Reliability, Validity, and Usefulness. *Review of Educational Research, 1971, 41,* 511-535.

Davis, R.H., Alexander, L.T., and Yelon, S.L. *Learning System Design.* New York: McGraw-Hill, 1974.

Hills, J.R. *Measurement and Evaluation in the Classroom.* Columbus, Ohio: Charles E. Merrill Publishing Co., 1976.

Kulik, J.A., and McKeachie, W.J. The Evaluation of Teachers in

Higher Education. In F.N. Kerlinger (Ed.), *Review of Educational Research, Vol. 3.* Itasca, Ill.: F.E. Peacock Publishers, Inc., 1975.

Popham, W.J. *Educational Evaluation.* Englewood Cliffs, N.J.: Prentice-Hall, Inc., 1975.

Sherman, T.M. Formative Student Evaluation of Instruction. Princeton, N.J.: ERIC Clearinghouse on Tests, Measurements, and Evaluation, 1975.

Sherman, T.M. An Evaluation Model for Judging the Quality of Instruction. *Journal of Instructional Psychology,* 1977, *4*(2), 21-29.

Sherman, T.M., and Winstead, J.C. A Formative Approach to Student Evaluation of Instruction. *Educational Technology,* 1975, *15*(1), 34-39.

The Following Are Some Texts Covering Evaluation and Measurement

Copperud, C. *The Test Design Handbook.* Englewood Cliffs, N.J.: Educational Technology Publications, 1979.

Ebel, R.L. *Essentials of Educational Measurement.* Englewood Cliffs, N.J.: Prentice-Hall, Inc., 1972.

Gronlund, N.E. *Constructing Achievement Tests.* Englewood Cliffs, N.J.: Prentice-Hall, Inc., 1968.

Karmel, L.J. *Measurement and Evaluation in the Schools.* London: The Macmillan Company, 1970.

Lemke, E., and Wiersma, W. *Principles of Psychological Measurement.* Chicago: Rand McNally, 1976.

Lien, A.J. *Measurement and Evaluation of Learning.* Dubuque, Iowa: Wm. C. Brown Co., 1976.

Popham, W.J. *Criterion-Referenced Measurement.* Englewood Cliffs, N.J.: Educational Technology Publications, 1971.

Rahmlow, H.F., and Woodley, K.K. *Objectives-Based Testing: A Guide to Effective Test Development.* Englewood Cliffs, N.J.: Educational Technology Publications, 1979.

Wordrop, J.L. *Standardized Testing in the Schools: Uses and Roles.* Monterey, Calif.: Brooks/Cole Publishing Co., 1976.

Part VI: Remediation

14

Remediation

The purpose of remediation is to take advantage of evaluation data to revise and improve the effectiveness of instruction. Remediation is the process of analyzing evaluation data to identify problems and to make revision decisions to correct these problems. Remediation activities must be tied directly to instructional outcomes on both quality of instruction and student learning from instruction. This is a complex process. That is, remediation necessitates the examination of the entire instructional program in order to identify components of instruction which may be altered to improve outcomes. Decision-making is involved in remediation, which frequently will require information in addition to that collected during assessment and evaluation.

In this chapter, we will delineate the characteristics of effective remediation; identify the types of data needed to engage in remediation activities; and discuss decision-making during remediation. The chapter will begin with a brief discussion of the rationale for remediation and an explanation of the process for conducting remediation.

Rationale
If perfection were attainable, then remediation would be unnecessary. However, no instructional program can be perfectly successful 100 percent of the time with all students. That is, almost always instruction will fall short of being completely responsive to students. This may show up in two ways; either problems attributable to the quality of the instructional program or problems associated with student achievement.

One of our basic premises has been that instruction should be responsive to student needs. Therefore, when students do not learn as expected, the problem lies in the lack of responsiveness of the instruction. It may appear, then, to be a contradiction to separate remediation activities into two categories. The distinction, however, is important and primarily a matter of degree of the identified problem.

That is, we need to focus our attention on both the quality of the instruction and student achievement. Instructional quality is ordinarily a relative judgment based on achievement across all students. Student achievement, on the other hand, is individually based, regardless of how the group has done as a whole. We will deal with these two separately in detail later. The following is intended to set the conceptual framework for establishing each category as important.

Remediation, or improvement of the instructional program, is a major goal of an instructional designer. No instructional program should be considered beyond further development or refinement. The decision on what improvements need to be made should be based on data gathered during evaluation. When these data indicate relatively widespread problems, the problem areas need to be further defined. The focus is on the identification and specification of instructional components when decisions have resulted in instruction which is unresponsive to many students. In other words, instruction which has resulted in many students experiencing learning difficulties must be revised. Remediation with individual students is another matter. It is necessary at times to revise instructional decisions for a single student in order to make the instruction more responsive to that student's needs for the particular learning involved. Modifications of this sort are transitory in that they are unique to the student. They are not widespread enough to warrant a revision of essentially successful instructional decisions.

The teacher is faced with making decisions about the severity of the unresponsiveness of instruction. Remediation decisions should be based on both formative and summative evaluation data. In some cases, this may require a major modification of instructional decisions. In other cases, substantive changes will not be necessary; instead, modifications which impact only a single learner will be made. Attention to remediation, like evaluation, is an ongoing process that begins at the point of the first instructional exchange.

Let's look at this process in terms of teacher actions and decisions. Following the analysis of evaluation data, the teacher must ask questions about the quality of instruction and the level of student learning. When either or both are found wanting, remediation begins. The process is one of systematically reviewing instructional decisions to identify problems on a component-by-component basis. The first step in this process should be to isolate problem areas by major components. The results will ordinarily be a series of general hypotheses by the teacher concerning where problems may have occurred. The second step is to investigate these hypotheses and refine them into specific problem hypotheses relative to actual decisions within each sub-component. The goal is to answer two basic questions: "What decisions resulted in teacher actions which were unresponsive?" and "Why were these decisions unresponsive?"

Doing this requires additional data and a more careful analysis of the evaluation data gathered. Additional data may be sought in a number of ways, such as through diagnostic testing, observation, interviews, and questionnaires. These data may then be used to pinpoint problem areas and provide information for generating alternative teacher actions, which will resolve identified problems.

The inclusion of remediation as a major component in responsive instruction implies a willingness on the part of the teacher to stick with the problem until it is solved. It is a stance of assuming responsibility for instructional decisions with the realization that any decision may not be the best. That is, we are accepting our fallibility as instructional decision-makers and seeking ways to learn from past decisions and improve future decisions.

One final note on the relationship between the evaluation and remediation components: Data gathered during evaluation can facilitate remediation, if these data are designed to do so. Therefore, evaluation should be developed with remediation in mind. For example, if the goal of instruction was to teach addition, the learning of addition could be evaluated by having students add. One way to do this might be to have students record their sums on an answer sheet. This would yield a score of correct and incorrect responses indicative of student learning. However, such data would contribute little to remediation. It may be more useful to require students to work out all problems during evaluation and indicate the process they used by doing all computational notes on the evaluation instrument. As a result, the teacher would have sufficient information to identify probable process problems, such as not carrying numbers correctly.

Recall that one of the purposes of evaluation was to identify learning problems so that these could be remediated. This means that evaluation should be carefully constructed so that the learning process is exposed in order to identify learning gaps. This should be a consideration with both formative and summative evaluation.

Remediation of Instruction

The instructional program is the focus of remediation when it is discovered that many students are not learning as expected. When this occurs, we can assume that the instruction was not responsive to student needs. The basic problem here is to make a decision about the adequacy (quality) of the instruction. There are two general possibilities:

1. There may be a major problem with decisions in one or more components which affect all students.
2. There may be a major problem with decisions in one or more components which affect students with a certain set of aptitudes or characteristics.

If it appears that all or a majority of students experience the same difficulty, then a major revision of the instructional decisions responsible for the difficulty is necessary. The first step in effecting this revision is to identify which decision is the probable cause. This should be begun by examining the learning deficit in terms of what knowledge, skills, concepts, etc., are necessary to acquire the learning in question. Following this analysis, the teacher should generate some hypotheses related to the major components of the instructional model. Note that these hypotheses should be related to instructional features, not to student characteristics. The purpose of this hypothesizing is to attempt to narrow problem areas to one or more major components. If this is not possible, then all major components and sub-components must be equally examined.

At this point, the focus of investigation should be on the two questions presented earlier: "What decisions resulted in teacher actions which were unresponsive?" and "Why were these decisions unresponsive?" These questions must be posed to each and every specific instructional decision in the relevant components. The attempt is to pinpoint specific decisions which were unresponsive. Additional data will probably be needed to determine the source of learning difficulty, including data from students in response to questions, such as "Why do you think you failed to learn this?," and data from empirical studies and a rethinking of the logic used to arrive at the instructional decisions in question. Essentially, the teacher has turned into a detective in search of clues to explain the learning problem identified.

Once these data have been generated and analyzed, the teacher is ready to make new decisions. A new set of alternatives should be generated and analyzed and a decision made on a new set of teacher actions. The revisions should then be tested out with students and incorporated into the instructional program.

If it appears that the problem is isolated to a group of students with similar aptitudes or characteristics, essentially the same procedure should be used. However, the purpose would be to add to the instructional program some alternative instructional decisions which would be responsive to this constituency.

Even successful instructional programs in which no major problems have been identified should be considered for remediation. Remediation in such situations would constitute "fine tuning" instructional decisions. Evaluation data may yield information which indicates general areas where improvement could be effected (e.g., "What did you like least about this course?") on summative student evaluation. Frequently, successful students can supply valuable information on how instructional decisions can be improved.

Remediation of Individual Learning

Students are likely to experience learning problems at any point in the instructional program. These learning problems are reflected in evaluation data; and, if severe enough, remediation should be pursued. Learning difficulties may be the result of:

1. Unresponsive decisions on one or more components.
2. A transitory learner state which affects learning.

The initial action in remediation should be to determine to which general area the problem belongs.

If the learning problem appears to be associated with a transitory learner state (e.g., illness, temporary heavy work load in other studies, etc.), then little needs to be done in the way of providing alternatives. In situations such as these, we can assume that the student essentially never interacted with the instruction. The best course of action is to have the student repeat (or, more accurately, attempt for the first time) the instructional program. It is, of course, possible that the student will experience real learning problems involving unresponsive decisions during the attempt to master the material. If this occurs, then remediation of the sort described below is in order.

When it appears that decisions which were not responsive to student needs are the cause of lack of achievement, a remediation process similar to that described for instructional remediation must be begun. This is a complex process of examining specific instructional decisions to identify specific changes which will result in greater student learning. Since we are dealing with one or only a few students, the process is usually relatively informal and involves no intentions to modify the instructional program in a major way. This process applies to both formative and summative evaluation results.

The first step is to analyze the learning error and generate hypotheses regarding probable major components to which the unresponsive decision(s) may belong. These hypotheses should then be investigated with the student(s) in order to identify specific decisions which resulted in unresponsive instructional actions. The best way to do this is usually to interview the student about the general nature of the problems experienced. Once these data are acquired, they should be analyzed in an attempt to pinpoint specific instructional decisions which may require change. The focus of these activities should be to respond to the questions, "What decisions were unresponsive?" and "Why were these decisions unresponsive?," for each instructional decision included in the general hypotheses.

Additional data will then be required to specify the exact decisions which resulted in unresponsive instructional features. This will involve further investigation of student learning problems. Following an analysis of these data, a new set of alternatives should be generated and narrowed to several choices. The student(s) involved may then be included in the final decision on a course of teacher action. These students should then be recycled through the altered instruction.

Research on Remediation

The description of these remediation activities may make them sound overly complex, cumbersome, and detailed. The remediation process *is* complex; however, the majority of the actual remediation actions occur in concert with one another and follow naturally from one to the next. It appears relatively clear that successful remediation includes a great deal of attention to problem identification and the expenditure of large amounts of resources in corrective instruction. We can assume, then, that remediation is going to require both time and effort and that the overall instructional design should be constructed to accommodate these remedial activities.

There are, of course, a number of ways remediation may be planned. A branching program is one example of organizing material to be responsive to student errors. Essentially, a branching program [a form of programmed instruction (see Markle, 1969)] provides students with different instructional sequences based on students' responses to formative evaluation. Remediation may also be organized around the use of parent aides, teacher aides, peer tutors, and cross-age tutors, when teacher time is largely occupied in instructional delivery and evaluation.

Numerous reports exist on the impact of remedial programs or programs that are designed to upgrade students who are below specified levels of achievement (for those interested in reports on these programs, ERIC, the *Current Index of Journals in Education,* and the *Education Index* carry descriptors, such as remedial programs, compensatory education, and intervention, which will include reports of programs of this sort).

In general, all of these programs are characterized by highly structured assessment procedures, intensive and individualized diagnostic testing, concentrated and individualized instruction, and extensive evaluation on a number of dimensions, usually including academic achievement and attitude.

Remedial programs cover practically every content area, though they are associated usually with basic abilities, such as communication skills, reading, and math.

Age may be an important student dimension to consider when planning remediation with younger children and early adolescents. For example, Dietrick (1972) found that age was a dominant factor in the success of remedial programs designed to foster reading ability. Older children profited more than younger children from remedial activities. This may not be surprising from a developmental perspective, since the younger children may have experienced problems due to slower development of native abilities. Without such abilities, it may be impossible to aid these students other than to continue to challenge them with readiness activities.

Bloom (1974) and his colleagues have been interested in remediation. An important point they make is that remediation should not consist of simply recycling students through the *same* instruction. Recycling students through the same learning activities in which they were originally unsuccessful is likely to be unproductive the second time as well. This point is clearly in line with the responsive instruction emphasis on identifying and changing instructional decisions which were not responsive to student learning needs. Block (1971) also pointed out the advisability of providing students with a series of alternatives for remediation.

Bloom (1974) spent considerable time justifying the benefits of immediate correction of non-mastery. His conclusion was that the effort expended to correct learning problems as they occur saved time in the long run, since *"early* learning units contribute to the student's better motivation and improved cognitive entry behaviors (prerequisite learning) for the later learning units in a sequential series" (p. 685). Bloom went on to contend "that a particular amount of time and help at an early stage in the learning sequence has a different effect than an *equal* amount of time and help at a later stage in the learning sequence" (p. 685). An analysis of the expense involved in most remedial or compensatory programs appears to support Bloom's contention.

It is not possible to stop an ongoing instructional program to resolve the learning problems of a few students. In addition, in most cases, teachers do not have the wealth of resources necessary to mount an intensive attack on learning problems. However, it does appear that effective remediation requires extensive diagnostic information and additional resources. To the extent that these data and resources can be included in the original design of instruction, the easier it will be to remediate learning problems. That is, remediation should be explicitly designed and considered an integral part of instruction. If remediation is approached in this way, rather than as an afterthought, much of the data and resources necessary will be available when remediation is necessary.

Decision-Making

Decisions in the remediation component can have a great impact on student achievement. When failure is detected, it is necessary to identify, analyze, and modify instructional decisions which resulted in the failure to learn. In effect, remediation requires instructional decisions about instructional decisions. The development of these decisions emanates from a process of questioning previous decisions, analyzing these decisions, generating new data, analyzing these data, generating new alternatives and decisions, and evaluating these new decisions. The exact nature of the activities within this process cannot be specified. They rest on the instructional decision-maker's willingness to seek out learning problems associated with instructional decisions and to modify these to be more responsive to student learning needs. It appears that the effort necessary to conduct remediation is worthwhile and productive for both teacher and student.

Summary

Remediation is the complex and ongoing process of seeking out and "fixing" instructional features which are unresponsive to student needs. The process should begin at the point of the first instructional exchange and continue throughout instruction in reference to both summative and formative evaluation. The focus of remediation is on instructional decisions, since this is where teacher control lies. The goal of remediation is to insure student learning by making either major or minor modifications in instructional decisions.

References

Block, J.H. Operating Procedures for Mastery Learning. In J.H. Block (Ed.), *Mastery Learning: Theory and Practice.* New York: Holt, Rinehart, and Winston, Inc., 1971.

Bloom, B.S. Time and Learning. *American Psychologist,* 1974, 29(9), 682-688.

Dietrick, C. Changes in Reading Achievement, Perceptual Motor Ability, and Behavior Adjustment as a Function of Perceptual Motor Training and Individualized Remedial Reading Instruction. Final Report. Office of Education, 1972.

Markle, S.M. *Good Frames and Bad.* Second Edition. New York: John Wiley and Sons, Inc., 1969.

Part VII: Conclusion

15

Conclusion

Responsive instruction has been presented as one way of organizing teacher decision-making. It is clear that teacher decisions are frequent and important; what is not clear is how these decisions are made ordinarily by teachers. Responsive instruction provides a framework for making decisions about the design of instruction in an informed, conscious manner. This is accomplished, first, by identifying the major decisions which must be made and, second, by gathering together the relevant empirical information and logic necessary to make decisions. Instruction has been portrayed as a decisive activity, the success of which rests in large measure on the teacher's ability to make good decisions.

Responsive instruction is, however, more than a recipe for making necessary decisions. It is essentially an approach to designing instruction and to solving instructional problems. Responsive instruction is based on the notion that instruction will be most effective if instructional decisions are made in conformance with the aptitudes and characteristics of learners. That is, the content and teacher action involved must be responsive to the needs of learners. Making instruction responsive requires a thorough knowledge of the learner, the content, and possible teacher actions. With this sort of understanding, the teacher has the necessary ingredients to implement a strategy for making effective instructional decisions.

Thus, we can consider responsive instruction as a way of thinking or an approach to instructional design characterized by the following elements. First, the learner is always the prime focus of every decision. Second, decisions are made in an informed and conscious manner. Third, to the extent possible, decisions should be based on empirical evidence and/or an explicit decision-making framework. Fourth, decision-makers are not infallible. We cannot specify what will "work" every time; and, in some cases, even the most informed and well-considered decision will not result in success. This lack of success, though, is seen as an opportunity to gain new knowledge and produce other, hopefully more successful decisions. Finally, the teacher/instructional designer is the ultimate source of responsibility for all decisions over which he or she has control.

It seems reasonable at this point that some perspective be given to these ideas about teacher decision-making.

Making instruction a practical and realistic enterprise requires consideration of the real problems and opportunities which exist in any situation. There are no formulas for doing this. The best that can be done at this time is to point out the advantages of thinking about instruction in a systematic manner. At a minimum, a teacher who utilizes such a framework will be aware of what decisions need to be made and how he or she is to make them. As a result, the important role of decision-making is not forfeited (Farr and Brown, 1971) and made by default by textbook writers or others. At a minimum, then, the teacher has control over what happens in the instructional situation. There are other advantages which have been mentioned earlier, such as being able to revise when necessary, being able to choose where to focus effort, and being able to justify what is going on. However, the basic issue appears to be one of being in real control of instruction.

Responsive instruction provides this kind of framework for making instructional decisions. The framework, however, may be of little practical use, unless a substantial effort is made to utilize the framework as a strategy for designing instruction. Our use of strategy here conforms to what Gagne and Briggs (1974) called a cognitive strategy. That is, it is a way of thinking about or a strategy for evolving instructional designs. The essential element is to live up to the intent of the strategy and to try it out repeatedly until you become comfortable with it, or abandon it as not appropriate for you. In other words, it is necessary to give the approach a fair trial by using not only the framework but also the underlying basis of the framework. For responsive instruction, this is to approach the design of instruction as a holistic enterprise, fully informed, and with a willingness to modify and revise decisions until a successful outcome is reached. Through careful planning and consideration of the variables identified, the probability of success is increased. But instruction is also a human enterprise and subject to human error. The goal is to do the best possible under the given circumstances with a well-specified ideal situation in mind. While the best we can imagine is not always possible due to circumstances beyond our control, it is always possible to seek out what is "best" in a given situation by making decisions systematically and being willing to evaluate, revise, evaluate, revise, etc., until you are satisfied with the instructional program. It is this willingness to learn from past decisions, evaluate, and revise which characterize the substance of responsive instruction.

In the remainder of this chapter, we will review two issues which impact on the practicability of responsive instruction. The first is the multitude of decisions necessary in designing and delivering instruction. The second is the notion of equal educational opportunity as applied to instructional programs.

Decisions, Decisions

We have continually spoken about making decisions and have identified specific decision-points. The overall impact may be that this is just too much to expect of one teacher or that an inordinate amount of time and effort is required. Teachers and instructional designers are expected to deliver on a regular basis and with great frequency, often at a minimum of five class sessions per day. It seems that the necessary planning time is just not available.

This is a good point, and it is clear that a teacher can do only so much. How much is enough is obviously an individual decision. It is necessary, however, to have an ideal in mind in order to approximate the best practical situation. A well-defined structure is one way to establish such an ideal. Such a structure provides a goal toward which to work. Practically, such a structure provides a solid basis for making decisions about what decision to make. That is, it allows the teacher to determine where to focus effort or where available energy will be most profitably spent.

Good instructional programs are not developed quickly. A good instructional program is developed slowly and systematically through careful evaluation and research. The same approach can be applied to the design of classroom instruction by individual teachers or instructional design groups. The idea is to choose where to place developmental efforts and to focus attention on decisions in these areas. For example, it could be decided that special emphasis needs to be placed on the structure of learning. Subsequent efforts could then be devoted almost exclusively to these decisions. Once these decisions are solidified, then it is possible to move on to other decisions.

An instructional program may be seen as evolving from selective efforts into a fully developed program over time. This appears to be a realistic approach in most instructional situations. Most teachers are responsible for teaching the same subject matter time after time. Thus, it is entirely possible to begin the process of conscious decision-making within one or two components and gradually to expand the sophistication of the program as time and resources allow. In effect, the teacher can plan the development process to suit the demands of the situation.

Decisions about where to begin the process are situational and will vary. Some factors which might influence this decision are the needs of students involved, the abilities of the teacher, the time and resources available, and the current status of the instructional program. This is an important area of teacher control which is often overlooked; however, teachers clearly have the responsibility and opportunity to determine what decisions they will make and when these decisions will be made. These may be the first, and in many ways, the most important decisions that a teacher can make in establishing control over the design of instruction. Doing so obviously requires a well-formulated decision-making framework.

Equal Educational Opportunity

Educators, sociologists, politicians, and legal experts have been concerned with the equality of educational opportunities in the United States in an intense way for at least 25 years. Most of this concern has been directed toward the equality of educational opportunities available to minority ethnic groups. In general, equal opportunity has been defined in terms of resources available and the outcomes produced from these resources. Barr and Dreeben (1978) pointed out that this approach is one borrowed from economics, called production function. "When the concept of production function, taken from economics, is applied to the study of school effects, the school is treated as a firm which transforms inputs (such as books, teachers' time, activities, physical plant, and equipment) into outputs (such as increments of knowledge, change in attitude, or gains in achievement)" (Barr and Dreeben, 1978, p. 90). The majority of analyses have concentrated on the overall effects resulting from aggregates of resources within educational systems.

Our concern with equal opportunity is a bit different in that we are more concerned with the real opportunity to learn which is available to each learner. The production function implies the transformation of a raw material into a desired product at the least possible cost. Teachers, unlike industrialists, have special demands placed on them due to the nature of the raw products (students) with which they must work. The industrialist seeks out and selects the raw products which may most economically be transformed into the finished product. Teachers must accept their raw products as they are. The industrialist selects raw products to conform to the manufacturing process. The teacher must make the process conform to the raw products.

As a result, regardless of the resources available, if these resources are not responsive to student needs, they are essentially being wasted. The task of the teacher is to make the resources or instructional process responsive to student needs. Thus, our concern with equal opportunity is not with the allocation of resources but the differential utilization of resources such that they meet the differential needs of learners.

The task is a large one, because students present a vast array of differential needs. These include social needs, emotional needs, intellectual needs, and physical needs which contribute to an individual learner's opportunity to learn. Real opportunity to learn is essentially an individual phenomenon based on meeting the needs of the learner involved. The only way to equalize learning opportunity is to arrange instruction such that it meets the unique needs of each learner. This obviously does not mean that each learner receives the same instruction but that the instruction each learner receives is adjusted to suit him or her. Equality of opportunity is achieved by making the instruction each student receives responsive to that student's needs.

We must again face the issue of practicality. How practical is it to provide equally responsive instruction to every student? The issue is not dichotomous; rather it is a matter of degree. As indicated earlier, instruction can be developed over time such that an increasing number of components are made more and more responsive. This can be done by providing alternatives within components from which students can choose or be directed to the alternative best suited to them. Or, second, it can be accomplished by specifically organizing instructional decisions to suit the needs of each individual student. The goal in both cases is to increase real learning opportunities to the greatest extent possible.

Regardless of the way in which increasingly equal opportunities are developed, it appears that a well-defined process is necessary in order to make equality practical. That is, one must be able to first identify the dimensions on which instruction may be equalized and, second, be able to make decisions on how to equalize opportunity. Responsive instruction provides the necessary framework for such decisions. Whether or not the decisions are made which result in equal opportunities. is the responsibility of the teacher.

A Final Note

Teacher planning and decision-making can be guided by structural approaches, such as responsive instruction. When this is the case, decisions are made roughly in a sequential order, one at a time, until the instructional design is completed. However, for students, the impact of all these decisions is immediate and continuous. That is, once the student begins to interact with the instructional program, he or she experiences every decision at one time. At this point, instruction is not a sequence of well-considered and thoughtful decisions by a teacher but has the impact of a total experience. To the extent that the design decisions hold together as a holistic system, the instruction should be perceived as a unified entity. This holism can only be achieved by clearly conceptualizing instruction as something more than a series of independent decisions or a sequence of roughly, but ill-defined, teacher actions. Each decision must be considered in terms of its relation to other decisions so that all actions fit together into a total experience. The resulting instruction, designed from this perspective, should be a well-organized system which is success oriented and practical because it has been designed to be so.

References

Barr, R., and Dreeben, R. Instruction in Classrooms. In L.S. Shulman (Ed.), *Review of Research in Education, Vol. 5.* Itasca, Ill.: F.E. Peacock Publishers, 1978.

Farr, R., and Brown, V.L. Evaluation and Decision-Making. *Reading Teacher,* 1971, *24,* 339-344.

Gagne, R.M., and Briggs, L.J. *Principles of Instructional Design.* New York: Holt, Rinehart, and Winston, Inc., 1974.

Glossary

Adaptive Instruction—instruction designed to accommodate individual differences in learners.

Aptitude—any characteristic of a person that forecasts his or her probability of success.

Aptitude-Treatment Interaction (ATI)—the differential effects which accrue from a single treatment or instructional program on learners due to variations in aptitude.

Assessment—the process of gathering decision-making information about students.

Content Components—the analysis of content outcomes into component parts using an organized analysis system.

Content of Learning—the process of analyzing goal statements into content components.

Content Outcomes—classifications of learning outcomes or goal statements into types of learning according to an organized classification system.

Control—the ability to manipulate instructional variables.

Criterion-Referenced Test—the evaluation of learning outcomes against a predetermined standard or criterion.

Decision-Making—the systematic process of identifying and defining intended outcomes, generating alternative solutions, selecting an alternative to reach the outcome, and evaluating the results.

Evaluation—the process of determining the effects of instruction; or the comparison of actual outcomes with intended outcomes.

Formative Evaluation—evaluation conducted during the delivery of a program with the purpose of improving the program.

Individualized Instruction—the conscious variation of specific instructional variables to conform to the learning aptitudes of each student.

Instructional Elements—the specifications of what the learner must learn.

Instructional Exchange—the interaction of teacher, content, and learner.

Instructional Variables—features of the instructional environment which are controllable.

Learning Conditions—the specific events which must be present for learning to take place.

Learning Processes—the analysis of content into instructional elements.

Management—the purposeful maintenance of control over learner-content interaction.

Mastery—the achievement of objectives by a learner; or the achievement of a stated instructional goal or objective at a predetermined level.

Message Channel—the sensory modality involved in communication.

Need—a discrepancy between a desired outcome and a current condition.

Needs Assessment—an organized effort to define the discrepancy existing between a desired outcome and a current condition.

Norm-Referenced Test—the comparative evaluation of learning outcomes among students.

Objectives—relatively specific statements of what students should be able to do following an instructional session.

Reliability—a relative measure of the degree to which information can be trusted.

Remediation—the process of analyzing evaluation data to identify learning problems, and making decisions to correct these problems.

Responsive Instruction—a systematic approach to making instructional decisions about the optimal arrangement of instructional variables to promote learning.

Strategies–specific actions taken by the teacher to effect the productive interaction of students and content.

Summative Evaluation–a general evaluation of the degree to which instructional goals have been met.

Task Analysis–the identification of different classes or types of learning outcomes.

Time–the instructional variable involving the rate of learning and the pace of instruction.

Treatment–any planned activity designed to produce a change in a learner or learners.

Validity–a measure of the degree to which a score indicates what the score is intended to measure.

Index

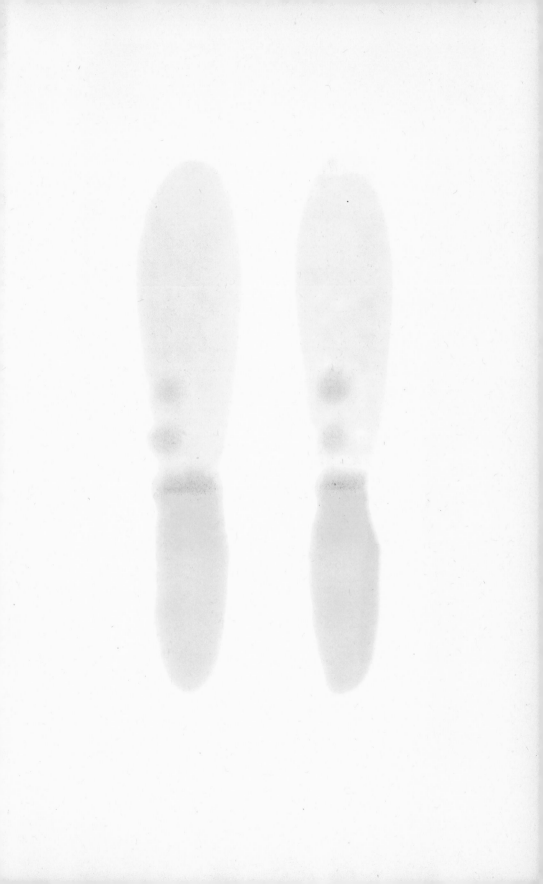